FOREVER FOR THE CULTURE

NOTES FROM THE NEW BLACK DIGITAL ARTS RENAISSANCE

STEVEN UNDERWOOD

BEACON PRESS, BOSTON

BEACON PRESS
24 Farnsworth Street
Boston, Massachusetts
www.beacon.org

Beacon Press books
are published under the auspices of
the Unitarian Universalist Association of Congregations.

29 28 27 26   8 7 6 5 4 3 2 1

This book is printed on acid-free paper that meets the uncoated paper
ANSI/NISO specifications for permanence as revised in 1992.

Text design and composition by Kim Arney

Library of Congress Cataloging-in-Publication Data

Names: Underwood, Steven, author
Title: Forever for the culture : notes from the new
Black digital arts renaissance / Steven Underwood.
Description: Boston : Beacon Press, [2026] | Includes bibliographical
references. | Summary: "Follows the construction of a new Black art
movement and how creators have defined a community when that
community does not have a physical space" —Provided by publisher.
Identifiers: LCCN 2025040037 (print) | LCCN 2025040038 (ebook) |
ISBN 9780807013380 hardcover | ISBN 9780807013397 ebook
Subjects: LCSH: African American arts—21st century | Art and the
Internet—United States | Arts and society—United States—
History—21st century
Classification: LCC NX512.3.A35 U53 2026 (print) |
LCC NX512.3.A35 (ebook)
LC record available at https://lccn.loc.gov/2025040037
LC ebook record available at https://lccn.loc.gov/2025040038

The authorized representative in the EU for product safety and
compliance is Easy Access System Europe 16879218, Mustamäe tee 50,
10621 Tallinn, Estonia: http://beacon.org/eu-contact.

CONTENTS

1

*Everyone wanna be black,
'till it's time to be Black.*

—A BLACK EXPERIENCE

LOG ON

I was six years old when I logged on for the first time. It was 2001, fresh after the Twin Towers fell on 9/11. There were plenty of pop-ups comparing President George W. Bush's IQ with just about anything to lure you into clicking.

At the time, the internet was an arcane world that made everyone an alien. We used a large box-like machine with a hump on its back to explore this world. We did not hold anything in this box, but it took up room.

It was made to be its own world with very few rules or regulations and little community. Or perhaps that is the concern conjured by the hysteria of Y2K—with its fads of fears pumped by a skepticism over technology and wars people could not hold so freshly after the recession of the early 1990s. For an adult nation that recently could not hold down reliable jobs, the suggestion of putting faith into virtual realities was comparable to caging lightning between your hands.

I invested time on many childish websites, which is to say I became aware of the value of time there. Online, you learn exactly how fast an hour is when twenty-four of those hours only went into a weekend twice. Online, you learn how much time you burn sleeping between long stretches of time trying to best scores that matter largely only to you.

And when you invest time this dramatically into any space, you find yourself being defined by it. In most skills, this would be called a craft at least, an art at most.

Ironically, I didn't make art on these childish games. And I'd never think of what I was doing wasting time on there as art. I'd call it "culture building." Those small things you do as a child where you fill the gaps of existing that adults expected you to leave empty before they too realize you are human: and that you exist outside of their own hawk-like purview. Those gaps of existing they hope to fill with a God, a religion, a class status, a race.

Eventually, you may learn to paint over those gaps to avoid disappointing an adult, though you sense they feel the clumps. As a child, the internet left some sizable clumps that could not be flattened by my family and what they knew Blackness to be as inheritors to generations of Black history, art, and culture. Those things contained in a book and given static, life-shattering word association like "Empowerment" and "Oppression" and "Colored" and "Nigga."

Just behind the Dell desktop in my grandfather's living room, behind the cracking pleather of our office chair, there was a bookcase. It couldn't have been more than eight feet tall, but as a child it stretched far up and up into the heavens. Its shelves were pregnant with encyclopedias from local salesmen, religious apocrypha snatched from Philadelphia yard sales, coffee-stained *Jet* magazines bound in twine, loose South Jersey R&B mixtapes, pimp manifestos, and old pulp paperbacks from the '70s: the kind of Black art that scorned bookstores and were traded with paper price tags between brown hands.

Books printed on the cheapest paper made gray by ink and elements bleeding into its skin through the years. It is an eternal moment that recalls everything Blackness was yesterday as far back as the literate Black soul. Such should be true for tomorrow as well.

In 2019, the spaces for Black folk to rest and roost on the internet were plentiful. By 2025, those places blinked out like starlight.

The internet and Black art triggered awe for completely different, profound reasons. Black art made me one-of-many, never myself. The internet made me myself all the time, one of many. No one would suggest finding the revolution on a blog or a chat room. It'd be years before teenagers were building profit off their hasty electronic art and chat logs. Nothing could be shared or dissected among a community without janky daisy chains of hyperlinks.

And if nothing could be shared, nothing could be compared; nothing could be granted value and heft. But Black art is always compared, shared, and given a value. It weighs the cost of one life with the lives chained to it even off the scale.

It did not usually feel preoccupied with my joy, though. Even as a Black person who smiled ear to ear when Black people fought for laughter with the mighty pressure of their jaws. I don't think Black art has taught me what joy is though, especially Black joy.

Joy is not a snack, but a meal. You chew on it to experiment with flavors. Roasty and savory like garlic butter before dessert, where fragrances can become an abnormal testament to a brief, unyielding safety. Joy invoking a memory of a home warm and wide and sheltering. Joy like a mother's bed. Like a father's shoes made of lived leather.

I could only know joy because of what I found online. It was hours uninterrupted with my race online that affixed me to what my Blackness had been trying to share with me just beyond all these troubles in us. It was solely what the internet was for.

To the chronically online, this does not sound like the world we know today. The chronically offline might not think there is much to a world of electricity behind our own.

Today, sharing a video is the most casual act of a neighbor—the most natural reaction online after shock or joy. Today, elections can be polarized by the news we suspect as true online despite the flaws of suspicion. Today's children are told a numerical formula to their worth.

Digital and tech journalist Taylor Lorenz expounds upon the influence of the digital space called social media in her book *Extremely Online*. "The rise of social media and the creativity of its users has given more people the chance to benefit directly from their labor than at any other time in history," she writes. "This expansion of opportunity has been particularly life-changing for many who have been historically shut out of legacy institutions. The creativity and tenacity of online creators has challenged traditional gatekeepers as never before, often with socially and economically liberating results."[1]

Lorenz was, of course, talking about all creators on social media creating a space and history for themselves. However, tucked within the crevices of this history, like always, are Black people and the things our experience plant and our politics grow. It is these moments that define Renaissance—many little artful seeds exploding into political jungles, such as the biome of the Harlem Renaissance.

In Harlem, artists arose, and they became Negro artists and Black icons. They holed up in smoky dens and brownstones tasting alcohol and drugs between shifts. In those brownstones, the icons scribbled about notepads and surrendered those eternal drafts to thin paper zines. All of these icons wrote and speculated on civil rights and the idea of Blackness resisting the world at large. They had a language for their identity that existed in their circles and outside of it. They could be surmised as artists of this age: the artists of the Harlem Renaissance.

Today, we've created new vocabulary that shapeshifts rapidly: Viner, TikToker, YouTuber, influencer, yapper, content creator. The concepts haven't changed, just the names. We're all artists: digital artists. As my grandmother used to say, ain't shit new under the sun except the folk smelling it.

I believe Blackness is traditional. We follow trends set forth by our cultural past.

My grandmother—Grandma Kandy Kane, named after the cane she walked with since the 1980s—taught me what Black art was growing up just after the Harlem Renaissance in Philadelphia, just 113 miles away from Harlem, NYC.

Deeply, she knew everyone in our family was like her, drawn to the arts by nature. She was a Catholic Black girl who could not knock the call of R&B, Motown, and Stevie Wonder. She snuck out the house and sung off-key to the kind of music that'd get the sin beaten out of you in a good Catholic household. She fell in love with the type of art bad Black girls swooned to and strived to understand why it was so bad to feel so loved in her own skin.

Why, she asked, was this sin of Black folk creating so much worse than the sins of any man—Colored or Caucasian? When she figured it out, she made Black music her business.

Her lessons for me suggested there is no way to be an artist while Black without speaking on Black people. Grandma suggested that Black people as a culture struggle with the world's racism in such a viscous and tactile way that despite the ways the world tries to invent passive synonyms for our trauma, the impact is all over our work. That's a frightening type of alarm for a certain kind of person.

Later in life, Grandma Kandy Kane became a devout Jehovah's Witness. She compared it to the "System of Things," a theological philosophy believed by Jehovah's Witnesses concerning the corruption of our social civilization. As a Black woman, she translated its principles to describe the universal suffering of Black people. She didn't have data to back it up or a background in study, but she lived in a racist existence; she knew.

And while my grandma suggested there is no choice but to be Black while being an artist, she knew there has always been a choice of whether or not to be revolutionary.

Personally, I do not think this ends as at just art. Socially, I find that Black people engage the world with a political mind. Our hair, our skin tone, our children, our culture, our speech are politicized in a new context every year.[2] It's easy to lie by denying the political in what we are. But it's a shame; it's not what we could consider conservative.

So, it makes sense that when we are online, we create explosions of politic. We look for oracles who can divine the shapes left in the aftermath's debris. We typically find those grand seers to look like us and have learned as we have: other Black people. And where we gather is a space no different than the smoking dens and the brownstone literati societies.

It is amazing that people think that there aren't such spaces where Black art can thrive in excess when there's a congregation like that. In Harlem, we only needed several long blocks and tall buildings to share the stories and skills that survived in the diaspora of our many tribes and bloodlines. It was an era before overwhelming adult literacy at that.[3] When we speak the same language in the same space, we could demand education from each other that transcended the convention of our upbringing.

Community can be anywhere, even if making community with everyone you find anywhere is dangerous. Black digital art is as real as we let it be. And what we let be is as real as our circumstances, because who would ever accept a reality like this if we were not conditioned to do it?

VIRAL

Like many in New York, I was willingly homeless.

Unlike too many of them, it wasn't a game of pretend for me. My family's chief source of safety came from my grandfather—a computer engineer who worked primarily in tech support and programming in

Philadelphia—who split his assistance across my uncle's entire family of five, my elder sister, and my grandmother, whose disability prevents her from seeking a lot of work since she fell through a Philadelphia sewer grate in the 1970s.

I came to New York that summer of 2018 with $1,200 in my bank account and blew $1,000 to secure a sublet on the Lower East Side that amounted to half of a basement split with an NYU grad. I bought an air mattress from Duane Reade and surrendered myself to pounding pavements to find my next quick dollar. I'd been training as a barista in Times Square at Blue Bottle Coffee—a job that would only endure a month as I became increasingly ill from a recently developed allergy to caffeine.

My first day, I wandered the neighborhood for six hours, willingly enslaving myself to the simmering New York summer. In the heat, New York turns into a stone oven, and the air turns red from the fire trapped within the concrete. I didn't feel at home here, no matter where I journeyed. New York was a city that felt sick down to its soul, a molded epicenter withering at its edges and surface with toxicity. Instead of leaving, I told myself that this was the culture I should expect. I sat at a café for hours, editing and submitting my résumé and cover letter to any New York position I could.

Total, I had maybe $1,900 in my account by the time August wound down into September, but I didn't have my next home. My body felt like I was lifting cinderblocks through water; nine hours of sleep didn't feel like an hour. The summer hit a high note when my subletter—a friend from high school—told me that I had to be on alert for the landlady.

"Yeah, we're not really allowed to sublet so just try to stay out of sight as much as possible."

This text confused me a little, not because I felt like it was an extreme deception, but because the walls already felt like they were closing in around me. Another anxiety was not going to help me feel stable. And yet this late notice came just in time as that very night, the landlady made a surprise visit and descended the stairs to the notice of no one screaming about a possible intruder.

She excitedly called downstairs to see if anyone was home. I was, but I couldn't say anything; my voice was several octaves deeper than my friend Morgan and his roommates. She came rumbling down the stairs. I've rehearsed last-minute reactions a lot in my youth, so my response was impulsive: I flew under my bed's covers and wrapped myself in a comforter just in time.

I had to be close to cocooned in my bed by the time she arrived in the basement. Morgan didn't share the favor of having the same skin tone as me. He's white. I'm Black. I'm a 4C. He's a 1B at best. No amount of New Yorker color-blind politics would deny this truly evident truth. The landlady would not mistake me for him if she saw even an inch of skin.

My breath slowed, but my heart was thunder in my ears. I could feel her vibrations beneath the darkness of my covers. Her every step was curious and frantic. She walked about for several minutes until deciding to go back upstairs. I didn't exit the covers. I stayed there, wrapped in darkness. Five minutes later, one of the roommates came home and had a conversation with the landlady: she said something about thinking an intruder was in the house. The housemates felt she exaggerated that to get into the apartment. I stayed under the blankets, even after Morgan's roommate came downstairs and told me we would be fine.

I fell asleep under those covers, thinking of the anxiety of the city and the history of Black art that preceded my late arrival. New York: the bedrock of so many cultures within Black culture. Almost thirty years before my arrival here, a Brooklyn boosting crew called the Lo Lifes stole Ralph Lauren articles from New York storeroom floors and brought High Fashion into the streets.[4] Nearly fifty years before my arrival: a basement party on 1520 Sedwick Avenue became the song of that street culture and people named it hip-hop.[5] Nearly a century before my arrival: the Harlem Renaissance's Black icons considered the new Negro and chiseled a tribe out of words, art, and song. This history was rendered a memory by that day. I did not hear many people speculating whether times like this might return either in popularity or potency.

The next day, I had to hide again as the room was toured by the landlady for a new tenant, hiding once more beneath my comforter as they did their browsing.

This life made me miserable. However, in terms of exposure and my art, I was breaking through the impenetrable sealing into the Renaissance no one saw coming. Not a cultural explosion of art and thought in a physical space though. Instead, it was one in a space of electricity and glass: the internet.

Somehow—I'd gone viral.

I landed my first great story on the back of a simple tweet on relationships.[6] It was an essay. I was irritated when I made the post, largely because the LES café I'd taken to frequenting to focus on my writing after my shifts slowly mutated into my primary criticism of liberal culture—gentrifiers who pretended to be different while calling the cops on the Dominican teens who walked in after work. This café had a German barista with a handlebar mustache who brewed an espresso with polished equipment and an eagle eye. Three tables away from him, two popular middle-aged YouTubers (white), a comedy duo, were discussing with business partners a sketch that reminded me of something I assumed was funny in the '90s. Not very engaging to me, but I assumed someone had to love it if these suits were willing to pay for it.

There was something repulsive as a Black artist in watching a couple so openly discuss everything Toni Morrison has done for women of all colors, then turn around and demand the manager toss out kids for disturbing their peace.

It was repulsive to be surrounded by the kind of carefree where you assume good things are owed to people when the right to a space to laugh at the sound of your own nonpolitical existence was not owed to children.

I maybe saw myself in these kids that has always existed in myself: the joy of a spontaneous moment of creation regardless of who is watching or what strangers feel obligated to in a space they've settled. Almost a century ago, Black faces, families, and friends raced across the nation like a bleeding scar to arrive in the North and claim the rightful inheritance denied to them for centuries. They arrived to face the same oppression popularized in the South; however, they now had access to different tools and resources to cultivate their pain and realities into artifice. At the time, they were thrown out of the mainstream, too, and pushed into social darkness. Today, they would be placed on white pillars and celebrated for being authentic and real to a Blackness those who dare to utter these words would never have a true idea of.

Like all writers in New York, I was trying to write a book. As Joan Didion said, that's what you do after you graduate as a writer—you write a book.[7] As a Black writer, I knew that meant that I had to finish a book while in school and have it ready for when I got out.

My time in that LES café was spent revising that book and querying as many agents as I could. I wrote essays on my time. I wrote poetry on my time. I pitched and networked and begged and bled for a chance to succeed eventually not only as a writer in New York City, but as a child of the Renaissance that made the city so great today. My birthright was denied to me, and those Dominican teens were sent home—no one had the honesty to actually address what was going on in front of us.

Everyone went back to their coffee. The couple in the café started explaining to one another how Toni Morrison could really open eyes about the gentrification problem in New York.

I folded this pain I was witnessing into myself, and it was present in me, a seed, when I took the time to unpack an issue that had nothing to do with whiteness at all. I was looking at Black men and how we enabled cheating in one another out of jealousy.

Twenty-four hours after the tweet, I'd gain 1,200 followers and was invited to write an article for *Blavity*—my first article postgrad for a popular publication. I was also able, to my surprise, to secure a follow from Viner Kenny Knox. I continued on an upward momentum throughout the remainder of August and used the time I spent in New York to finish up a functional portfolio of nonfiction work for an MFA application.

By the end of August, I left New York City with a persisting sinus infection. It was born from basement dust and haunts me as my ambitious sleep demon. Without a job, I moved back to South Jersey rather than brave the homelessness that felt imminent. However, my career as a writer did not stop. In fact, I found all my success outside of the space of touch, but digitally.

Most of the work in today's Black art is digital.

In this time, even as words touch this place, flattened brown fingers scroll and a video plays and keyboards tap. Whole experiences that once had no substance outside of the minds of the Black youths who suffered and celebrated them are converted into zeroes, ones, and utter lightning.

We of this era of Black art wake up when we feel like it'll help us most. Sometimes, that's at the ass crack of dawn, when brown skin looks most dry in blue light, and begin whatever we have to. Often, it's long after the sun has creamed its coffee—when the rest of the world, our audience, rises—that we choose to begin the crucial key to our creation: engagement.

I've read somewhere I cannot be troubled to remember because the author was white, Harlem was a time when time itself was too precious to be wasted. It was a period fresh after the culture of Black

Americans not yet known as Black, but Colored, moved on the time-table of the farms. Many Black pioneers in the 1920s were not primarily artists.

In Harlem, poets were chefs and bus drivers; musicians were servers and nannies. Comedians spent their days under the crushing weight of whiteness, and were told when and how to breathe—God forbid that their breaths be taken too loudly once or twice, and these comedians, Black men with families maybe bigger than a single income could sustain, lowering their heads to ensure a fiscal present. The only cohesive trend were the walls built on their families' corpses—"whites only" on the Black side.

I closed my eyes to visions of these juggernauts often in the basement of my sublet. The city-song of New York City drowned in a muffled clap. Darkness swirled above my head, and I saw my name spelled out S-T-E-V-E-N, with an inch between every letter to give weight, not for significance but because funeral parlors charge per letter. I wondered if I'd be buried with my words, and if those would be blessed by them long after this skin that defined so much of my earthly existence fell away, digested in the intestinal sac of the fastest critter in the underwood.

There's some audacity to imply there is a luxury in what happened to these artists. Without suffering, some say, there is no merit to artistry. White men have told me this. White men have told my mother this. I don't think these white men had any idea what they're talking about. But in a saccharine fashion, everyone has an opinion about what the Black experience should be like. It might be cute for white people to play games with wealth, and some truly might not be playing games—however, there is always more at stake for Black artists and entrepreneurs.

In 2019, it was reported that the average high wage of African American college graduates still is not enough to heavily impact the lifestyle experiences of Black millennials. This is largely because of the current trend of families of needs draining these children to survive. Black entrepreneurs send money to bankroll whole families and, quickly, even a $70,000 income becomes the standard paycheck-to-paycheck experience. I have friends who, within two months of beginning their first official job in their fields, bought the homes of their family members, putting the opening of their lives and independence on pause for half a decade to become the primary breadwinner of a household still insistently on treating them "in a child's place."

With this undeniable fact, there are those who argue there is a selfishness involved in pursuing the arts today. And, perhaps, since the early 2000s, it has been. The entertainment industry has historically barred Black artists from obtaining their dues and access that is as rightfully theirs prior to even the Harlem Renaissance, when the first artform pined for by the American African diaspora was simple English literacy. Christopher Priest, the writer attributed to making Black Panther "cool"—in fact, the first Black writer to work full time at Marvel in 1983—stopped his writing career to become a bus driver due to the increasing financial difficulty to maintain his arts career.[8]

In 2019, independent R&B singer Brent Faiyaz pulled back the curtain with uncharacteristic transparency on indie profits. In his manager's report, Brent Faiyaz sold out an LA show in twelve minutes flat; Faiyaz also only made $25,000 from streaming services in January 2019, a little more than minimum wage in some states. This income is on the back of around $30,000 in self-starter capital. This capital was pulled together by Faiyaz and his manager and becomes roughly $5,000 in gains without factoring the income made from touring. These numbers came after Faiyaz's team refused a $150,000 advance for an album following Faiyaz's 2018 successes.

Ultimately, the industry wasn't just interested in purchasing Faiyaz's name, but also roughly 82 percent of all of the music he released. The label would also handle much of Faiyaz's artistic development and direction, and if this relationship was not favorable in the way of Faiyaz post-signing, there would be very little that Faiyaz could do unless the label mutually agreed to dissolve their partnership—a turnaround that is rarely favorable for the label and, thus, rarely taken up. Thus, Faiyaz and other musicians are faced with a question that many Black artists of every era ask: Why continue with the industry standard of publication if it is very clearly so predatory? Why go mainstream?

Grandma Kandy Kane, a former music professional and manager who oversaw a wide variety of local entertainment contracts in New Jersey and Pennsylvania, had a lot of answers. My mother, a star performer of an all-girl rap group in the 1980s who opened for LL Cool J and a variety of artists who were on track to a record deal before my mother, to my grandmother's chagrin, became pregnant with my eldest sister.

My mother averaged around $300 per show, at four shows per month. My grandmother stated she spent over $50,000 on my mother total including licensing, clothes, travel, etc. These expenses were considered backbreaking and, without a label, would not spell much long-term success at all.

My grandmother broke down the logic of the business of entertainment between slicing onions and potatoes over a warming cast iron skillet. "[Labels] would handle more than just the large-scale finances. . . . [At the time,] they handled exposure too. You had to get your name out on a way larger scale if you wanted to sell anything." Of course, there existed an underground circuit in every city, but underground never actually spells more than an ironic hobby.

Philadelphia's underground rap scene has had many legends. I've more than a handful of memories of the random nights Black men, none older than I am today, huddled close in thick jackets over bullet wounds and tattoos, in the midst of the most intense cyphers I've ever seen. A lot of my person is convinced that is when I fell in love with Black Art—that moment their anger, so pronounced, erupted in a debate told in rhyme. Imagine my surprise when my older cousins called them bums and wanted to shoo them off the block.

Throughout the twentieth century, Black art—without the vital power of the mainstream—was just a hobby that consumed too much time, energy, and perseverance. That energy could be spent somewhere building a name backed by the only thing that should've been on Black folks' mind: money.

And yet here we are almost a century after the Harlem Renaissance; many brown-eyed Black students graduate high school and college into one of the most brutal American job crisis since the unemployment line hovered over 8 percent. In Ohio, where I spent the death of my boyhood, most Black and Brown men have a more realistic chance of attending college by joining the military than by any other means if they are not an athlete or of the top ranks in their high school; this "sacrifice" is often encouraged by academic professionals.

Black spaces were maybe the most impacted by this shift in the culture of economics. However, these digital spaces did not seem to suggest it. Financial reality is often presented as comfortable in an Instagram post, or a quick tweet where the reality of the artist is the commodity being sold. The truth is that no one wants to engage with a Black creative who does not at least seem to have their shit all the way together. It often comes at a shock when these creatives turn up on a feed with their lives significantly upended by the realities that was mostly veiled behind a well-maintained mirage.

However, in 2018, streaming changed everything; social media changed everything.

2

Do it for the culture.

—A BLACK EXPERIENCE

BLACK HISTORY

In 2013, five years before my first pilgrimage through the Schomburg Center for Research in Black Culture in Harlem, I kicked down the doors to Vine culture. I was late to the party after creating then deleting an account months prior when Instagram unveiled its video format. Since then, Vine had rebranded into an entertainment app with comedians, musicians, and general hobbyists. Influencers were making major money engaging in a vast array of content that Vine itself fed into by creating paid partners. Many of these greater faces, however, were not Black—a rising problem.

Five months before joining Vine, George Zimmerman was acquitted of murdering Trayvon Martin in Florida, leading to the international civil rights movement #BlackLivesMatter, as created by Alicia Garza, Patrisse Cullors, and Opal Tometi. This movement was pivotal, as it was the first time a movement was launched off the collective hive mind of Black people internationally standing together as a community on a digital platform.

Fresh off being expelled from Hiram College in Hiram, Ohio, for other racially motivated offenses, I found myself searching for answers in social justice. It'd been a month since I fully identified with feminism and progressivism altogether, and my Blackness in itself was radicalized by the combined work of Tumblr exploration of Blackness, Beyoncé's self-titled album, and pop-cultural discourse like *The Read.* I ran toward content that actively investigated Blackness. It's not that progressivism and feminism were not already unknown core aspects of my philosophy; rather, the word "feminism" always had an unsustainably white connotation to my upbringing that many in a Black household—a largely matriarchal enterprise—could not swallow. On Vine, I was fed Black trends and work largely through the small shells of community of underrepresented Black creatives and their higher-ranked creatives. Many were college students participating in decompression or content creation that amounted mainly to a part-time job or social clubbing. This was not unprecedented. Blackplanet.com, a social network for Black consumers that was *not* in fact Black owned, proved the substantial tendency of Black demographics to build community within digital cultures and spaces in 2008. This trend was only reinforced when then-senator Barack Obama launched his own Black Planet page during his presidential campaign bid. Prior to this, *WorldStarHipHop* became a hub for Black content, hip-hop media, and "viral pop" trends—or popular culture established from viral content.

However, over the course of two years, Vine culture, YouTube, and Twitter suddenly found a boom. Prominent Black creatives diversified their presence across multiple platforms, culminating in domination of the entire digital landscape. Previously, viral pop trends of Black communities were insulated and curated by niche websites or largely suppressed by algorithms, such as YouTube's then-controversial front page listings. Now, viral pop trends were intermeshed with general issues and concerns.

With the rising traction of #BlackLivesMatter and the rejection of the post-racial society as previously lauded by the Obama administration, Black art captivated social media's ever-growing platform and artists pushed their voices against the overcoming wave of hatred.

It's truth to say that Black art becomes its most powerful in reflecting the dangers of our existence. The Black Arts movement danced in the embers of the Civil Rights Movement, celebrating Black voices as what it was always meant to become: a community with its own existence that suffered pain and happiness bereft of white society, and those campaigning to obtain its same weight.

During this period, young Black lives were being terminated on a very public stage. Police brutality was the hottest topic of discussion on any neighborhood. Black parents and Gen X-ers simply observed the issue with ambivalence—business as usual in a culture where the police have always been likened to slave catchers and antagonism. My own mother, who'd been brutalized by the police in front of me and my two sisters when I was a child, shared much of this sentiment as she went about her business discussing the long history of racial atrocity that Black men and women faced when she was growing up in Philadelphia.

Black elders—grandparents and guardians to many—reacted with fear. Many of these elders compared their unease to their terror during the Civil Rights Movement and encouraged silence in their youth, rather than face to violence they sensed coming for anyone who was too vocal in their justified anger; after all, anyone can scream from the rooftops about injustice, all it'll do is make you the next target.

My feelings on the topic were different for a variety of reasons. As stated, in 2013, three months before Beyoncé released *BEYONCÉ*, the self-titled album, I was kicked out of Hiram College for an incident where I became accused of threatening to shoot a gun on a school campus. That morning, I was challenged with my first ever critical discourse on race and racial discrimination/objectification in which I defended a Wisecrack video's use of Ebonics and ethnic identity against what my peers were calling "ghetto" and relics of "unprofessionalism." The video's original goal was introducing literature by reimagining its package; that message did not reach the class.

After being brought to my college dorm, I was challenged with the existence of a tweet: "Shots fired in the halls and yes by me"—the tweet, without context, was dramatized as violent, particularly by the person who reported it to their RA. Though they found no weapon and I clearly explained the misunderstanding as colloquialisms intentionally misrepresented, I was arrested that very night by Ravenna Police Department and charged with causing false alarm, a misdemeanor. But I was sentenced to six months' probation in the city of Ravenna, Ohio, and a mandatory psychological evaluation and a restraining order from the town of Hiram, Ohio, where my college was located, effectively ending my college career.

What hadn't been discussed by the judge, police, or residential assistant was the truth of the matter: shots fired is a common bit of slang. The young woman—a mixed girl—who reported me and I had an ongoing issue with fits of anti-Blackness: where her perceived issues with her own Black parent would often manifest in vile and disrespectful slander against me and several other freshmen residents daily. On a few occasions, she accused me of gang violence. On more occasions, she talked about dark-skinned Black women in a negative light. One day, I had a proper moment to finally clarify some things about her behavior.

She didn't take kindly to the truth.

A day later, I'm arrested. Granted, there was time between this upheaval and my arrest where I did find this girl again and where there was another exchange in which she pursued me and accused me of another list of gang activity to justify her reporting. However, there is less justification in this action other than what was used as a basis for my arrest.

As the police officers handcuffed me for the first time in my life, I had many core-gutting realizations:

1. The first police officer thought he was protecting me when he told me to crush weaknesses of emotion as it rose to flood my eyes.
2. The second officer, who whispered that this was for the protection of my classmates, because he "knew about kids like me from Columbus" was but one face of the hydra of racism.
3. I placed so much emphasis on avoiding jail and going to college to justify a feeling of superiority over other Black men who were not as fortunate as I was, despite the world looking at us as the same; I enjoyed my little nook in the labyrinth forgetting I was also a lab rat chasing cheese.

My grandparents were wrong when they said nothing would keep me safe from police brutality and from racialized brutalities. My mother was wrong that the world held the same unsolvable opposition that she faced. This world, for Black people, was playing with a whole new set of rules in life's game where the only supposed rule is death. There was something about my eyes after this moment that held a stain of shadow, a shadow that could not leave any of my work. My poetry was all consumed with an aftertaste of sadness; my essays fixated on a cryptic sorrow, and my fiction always had the afterthought of horror—something that could not be escaped that could only be burdened, much like racism: much like Blackness.

I reflect upon this arrest with every hashtag I scrolled upon in the coming months afterward. It's a memory of pain that haunts. The haunting was laced in the work of many who would progressively adopt the name "content creator." Prior to these events, Black creatives were often boxed out of even mainstream digital happenings.

The likes of Tré Melvin, a popular and prominent Black YouTuber, weren't offered nearly as many opportunities for capitalization as his peers across the comedy landscape of social media and this was also true from other prominent personalities in the industry. And while these Black artists struggled often to make a name for themselves, the likes of Shane Dawson and Jeffree Star—two of the most successful names on YouTube—were making brands for themselves elevated by anti-Blackness (Shane Dawson infamous for using the N-word, making Black jokes, and wearing blackface and Jeffree Star using less than flattering language about Black women).[1] In a decade's time, both would become millionaires off the platforms they've built digitally without ever saying a word in the defense of many prominent Black artists and creatives struggling for the same access they used bigotry to cultivate.

In the mainstream, success was still being divided across a very limited pool of celebrities and creators. Film saw the creation of many Black materials, including *Twelve Years a Slave*, *Precious*, *The Help*, *For Colored Girls*, and *Fruitvale Station*, that received critical acclaim. There was a critical trend of Black experiences in pain that became a dominating criticism throughout the decade until, finally, works that hinged on this "exploitation" became akin to propaganda. Likewise, media that hinged too much on Black saviors risking their all for white people or fictionalized events of white saviorism for the disparaged Black communities were equally dissected, with Shonda Rhimes's *Scandal* receiving the brunt of this criticism at the time. Prominent Black producer and writer Tyler Perry was also scrutinized for his suspect portrayal of Black women and Black female self-indulgence in his work. However, within each of these works was a trend that went unaddressed: of current Black artists using film to bring Black experiences into its fullest fruition. Black pain, as awful as it is to experience, is the reality that is evident in our existence.

Entertainment can be a tool of escapism and representation; however, it is also the depiction of the awfulness of the human experience, and part of this awfulness is the misfortune that we become targeted due to our Blackness. Onne moment, we can become a president, a governor, a billionaire, or an astronaut; another moment, we can become victims of sexual assault, a police shooting, a lynching, or any amount of foulness. Largely due to the color of our skin or the contexts of our heritage. They despise us for our Blackness; how we're depicted is just a part of that constant struggle.

Black history shows that this isn't a new pain point. Authors like Toni Morrison were criticized by Black artists of her generation for her unabashed depiction of Black men and Black women in her work. Morrison's writing is often challenged for its subject matter, such as rape and incest. Some question if her novels' depictions of such things are rewarding for the Black community. However, around the time of these stories, my grandmother survived the sexual aggression of Black men in her community, including her very own father. Morrison's stories had not existed at the time of this abuse, and yet it happened. Were these Black men ever particularly concerned with how their actions were reflecting upon the Black man, an entity associated with rape and sexual depravity across multiple narratives?

Toni Morrison herself, a figure I had the honor of featuring in an *Essence* article for February 2019's Black History Now series, argued against the pretense that a Black existence should ever work to serve white narratives.

"I've had reviews in the past that have accused me of not writing about white people," she said in an interview with Charlie Rose. "I remember a review of *Sula* in which the reviewer said, 'This is all well and good, but one day she—' meaning me [Toni Morrison]—'will have to face up to the real responsibilities . . . and write about the real confrontation for Black people,' which is white people. As though our lives have no meaning and no depth without the white gaze. And I spent my entire writing life trying to make sure that the white gaze was not the dominant one inside any of my books."[2]

"The white gaze," she said. "It has nothing to do with who reads the books. Everyone, I hope, of any race, any gender, any country [reads my books], but my sovereignty . . . as a racialized person had to be struck immediately with [my] very first book."

Toni Morrison was influenced by African writers who assumed the centrality of their own race, because they owned their identity and they never seemed to have to justify their existence to white people. "In this country, [with] many books . . . you can feel the address of the narrator over my shoulder, talking to somebody else. They were explaining things that they didn't have to explain if they were talking to me."

FINDING BLACK TWITTER

In 2018, my sister, Corvetta, asked me how to join Black Twitter. I laughed. I laughed like celebration and vibrance. Like my lungs were expelling tuberculosis. I laughed for maybe longer than was probably comfortable, but such is the propensity for Black folk. Take a joy and make it last. Make it persist.

I laughed with the totality of Black thought. And I did so because of the size of the absurdity. As if Black Twitter was a thing you joined. You don't join joy; you create it with moments and people.

Such is the creation of a place where the many works of Blackness can be woven together: joy.

New folk to such an environment often confused Black Twitter with some great conspiracy. I swear, some imagine a dusty space of wooden skeletons in the butt of a brownstone that stinks of sweltering sweat, over-burned whiskey, and aluminum gin. Like spoiled limes in a wooden barrel bloated by ice chips half-past their prime.

Black Twitter is not a speakeasy.

Black space might be prohibited, but it is not prohibition.

This is godless country. Of sprawling usernames with subtle winks to something you ain't sure everyone knows much 'bout. Where everyone spells your name right on the first try and if not, the shade speaks for itself. Where most folk miss the point except the point they want to reach for. Of one stripper's journey with a white girl and her pimp boyfriend. Of X and his winding tales of hood heartbreak at 120 characters a minute.

My sister ain't the kind of girl who likes to look too hard for the answers right in front of her. That's not a bad thing. It's just a quirk of a personality with as many strengths as it has weaknesses. It means that if folk challenged her to find out something that isn't written down somewhere, she might never know.

For instance, Corvetta did not know that she already belonged to Black Twitter.

That's the beauty of places where Black folk congregate. They aren't places you can physically go. Black folk aren't used to owning much of anything in America. We mostly rent what we want and when we do own, there's too many walls around us. Couches touching both walls, knickknacks cluttering an armoire, tribal masks from a tribe with a suspiciously Irish name. We put things on too many shelves. My grandma Kandy Kane says that Black folk are allergic to buying furniture for our houses that actually fit there.

"Everything don't fit anywhere. It's like we thinks just because we got somewhere nice we gotta put as many nice things as we got in there. Keep the nice things there. Some shits gotta go. Some places just gotta just be."

When she said this, I knew she was giving me the Word. Black elders do that all the time. I think it's a remnant of our oral tradition outlasting even our education—teaching one another what it means to be a part of this tribe so far away from the Gulf of Guinea. Not lost. Never lost, but stubborn and cunning, talented at being together without ever whispering of unity.

We are descendants of a people with coded languages. Who sang songs in silent rebellion. Who trusted one another to know the words. Who tap into memory and subtext. Who preach. Who improvise. Who do because our gut tells us to. A field full of niggas who've done nothing—not piss or speak—for hours but hustle and sing; a field full of family who in verse know how many of their family they might never see again, and thank our God for it.

Corvetta belonged to Black Twitter because she knew at least three other Black people who know a song in our blood. And they know three other Black people who know the song in our blood. And they know a Black Brit who knows a different song in their blood, with a rhythm quite familiar. And they know kin across the waves who know three more. And we all know you don't disrespect your aunties and we know it's a shame how these kids run around acting all sorts of ways and how to be stubborn and how to sing—really sing—so the folk around you can't help but join.

The infancy of Black Twitter was nothing anyone who grew up on the internet can be surprised by unless they're lying to themselves, or they had no talent or inclination to get around the child safety filters on the desktop. There was no Black Twitter then; it was just twitter. Just like Black Vine was just Vine. Like Black Tumblr was just Tumblr.

Social media before Twitter's golden era was not capable of incubating what was necessary for true community. Twitter, as comedians mocked, was a place of pure thought and impulse. You said things because you had them on your mind and some people signed up to hear what you have to say. Before pictures. Before GIFs. Twitter was conversation and those who agreed or disagreed where the conversation had to go.

It was a thing of zeitgeist in every way something like Tumblr could be. And yet Twitter had not become that thing. Tumblr, at the time, was the place where liberalism and social justice warriors cut their weapons and their teeth on topic and conversation. Where other people could agree with you or flame war or do just about whatever it took to achieve an understanding of a thing that we hadn't known was called an "economy of attention."

But Tumblr didn't last forever. Twitter might not, but it lasted until the day I wrote this. Tumblr didn't die like Vine. In 2018, it collapsed in on the conversations surrounding whether people were ready to accept the fact folk are having sex on the internet, but that's a conversation for another time. Not another book. We'll get there. Don't rush me.

Twitter was there to catch them. It's probably the only refuge "situation" to work out that year. With a lot more sensitivity, even.

I mark the day the boat of Tumblr's first refugees brushed up on the shores of Twitter to be the day Black Twitter became a concept. It was the day folk so used to community and curating a space—the html source code of what the world is and what we would want it to be—decided that recklessness doesn't make a heart fonder.

We saw things: beefs and chaos and doom spirals. It'd been almost four years since #BLACKLIVESMATTER was scribed across the graphite tombstone of Trayvon Martin. We knew how to use our voice in a space of pure thought and reaction.

/////////

The first thing you notice about Twitter when you log on is that there's a lot of people talking all at once. Overlapping conversation is a skill set for most people of color, but especially Black folk. We are about the communal voice—that little moment where a child is outside a child's place and aunties are squabbling about some past wrong, they both keep getting details incorrect about and fathers against fathers who don't know so much, but they can prove they know more about something only they can be bothered to care for.

That half a second when the voices hit a pitch that sounds like the sharp bang of gunfire, when all of our history exists in the common consonant of love.

It is on Twitter where Viners call out the fact Vine knew it'd be dying, knew that it was not servicing those who bare the fruits of its trade: the content creators. Jay Versace, Demetrius Harmon (@ MeechonMars), and Kenny Knox (@KennyKnox) were some of the youngest creators on that app. They never dreamed of attending college or joining YouTube, because they were sure they could profit from Vine until the very end of their youth's springtime—which, for most men with clout and cash, could last well into their fifties.

However, the winter came when Vine announced it would be leaving us all. Then, there was a bit of time to jump ship before the entire thing went under the tide. It wasn't the first time we ever saw an app die. MySpace went first, but MySpace had its own util-ity of social media, teaching us how to speak to one another on not-quite-a-forum. Vine was unique that it was a station for entertain-ment outside of cable. Where people could get amateur content from people who might never know who they were. Where you could get content from people you might never follow. Where you could laugh or cry or learn or pry and not leave the four walls of your bedroom. And when such a thing dies a slow, painful death, bigger, older beasts show their fangs and swallow what part of the carcass it can get ahold of. Imagine having a leg before noon and by midnight it's clear across the country. You'll love your leg and know you can do something with it were you to find it in place somewhere along the lines, but for now it's gone. And you're left with the aching sting in a stump—waiting for someone to care to bring it back.

Soon, thousands upon thousands of cataloged materials vanished off the face of the app. Kenny Knox began hunting down Viner com-pilations just to find some of his classic videos. Demetrius "Meech" Harmon went into a depression and began releasing his own longer form content independent of Vine. It was the earliest days of Harmon's "You Matter" branding, which would later become a million-dollar brand, complete with a clothing line whose single recognizable slogan advocates for mental health and suicide awareness. Its hoodies have words of affirmation across the wrists, a not-so-subtle reference to patterns of self-harm that Harmon himself has been quite vocal about struggling with.

Harmon has never shied away from the fact his audience is many Black kids. Mostly those who have struggled with mental illness before the era focusing on mental health and awareness for Black people. Before 2016, a lot of conversations revolving around mental illness centered around shame and shied away from therapy. It often positioned questions of mental unwellness with spiritual uncleanliness.[3] "Get right with God and your mental health will get better."

Harmon's material never focused on the agony of this unwellness. Where harm rivets as a response to the wallowing, widening chasm in your being. Where joy sparks and extinguishes and sparks again, just to twirl on a wick and snuff out into wisps of vapor one more time. Not that the flame cannot return, or will not return, but that is the horrifying point: the spark will return and it will also go.

It's not a wonder that as Vine died and with it the need to chase joy as blank moments where joy is something you perform. When Meech launched his *You Matter* film, a short where Demetrius Harmon personifies his many mental illnesses, he was going to be speaking to a battle he recognized beyond himself. A niche of artistry that was not as overt as activism, but contained a constant conversation that his fans could engage with to normalize simply speaking on suffering in a way that wasn't so individual, and still quite personal.

It wasn't about Harmon's acting abilities, because in truth he was still blossoming as an entertainer, ore being melted down into raw material capable of being beaten and shaped into something a bit more upstanding. He might appear in music videos with Khalid, but from most people who could see he was learning that some crafts are not like the lightning he captured in his bedroom with an iPhone and a ring light—cataloging his humor between homework and homeroom. In truth, it was more about a word that would come to define this Black digital arts renaissance, and the generation of people who do not suffer unrealness. Authenticity, the art of weaving everyday life with glamour and spectacle, even if it dilutes what makes something, or someone real.

Online, authenticity is where conversations exist on the fourth dimension, where time doesn't exist and most conversations are as omnipresent as attention. It is profitable too. Because everything on the internet is an advertisement, which means everything on the internet can put coin in the pockets of an authentic enough personality.

Other eras were not like this.

When I think of Harlem, I think of the bizarre crampedness of it all. Harlem is huge, when you walk it, but it is far smaller in memory. When you think about the names, you come away with a handful. I believe that we have forgotten more names than we remember. Perhaps it is intentional. Perhaps it is because when no one is worried about writing down today, they will not write down important history and the people who did not submit become just another implication before the final punctuation in a sentence of a topic.

And when I think of the Black Arts movement, I think of how much the world has tried to make me forget it. It is the era where people remember the most, because people were documenting everything. Nikki Giovanni on soul!!! Telling James Baldwin to lie to her, Toni Morrison remembering the vitriol her peers had for her truth-telling; Maya Angelou becoming the mechanism of civil rights and a juggernaut of multifaceted identity.

Never once did we say "money." Of course, there were pockets of wealth in other eras, but nothing related to the arts becoming commodity. And, sure, I am never one to wager against what one can do as the poster of one nature or another, but in this era of digital art, in a society that cosplays post-racial creation, money trades Black hands faster than most rivers still flow. We see the overnight exchange of tax brackets. We see art transforming into commerce and never reverting back. We see a culture around a fast-paced pedaling of identity that cannot end until one's own audience widens its jaws and crunches the creator into consumption.

On the timeline, folk talk about Beyoncé not owing us nothing from her personal life. Vulnerability is owed to no one. Artists argue, what is the point of creating if you will not be vulnerable with it? If it isn't sometimes ugly, disgusting, sloppy, and rude? If it isn't sometimes horrifically narcissistic and benevolently oblivious? Then it's just a product. Art without vulnerability is just product.

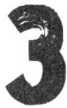

If I'm not the gifted, why am I Black?

—A BLACK TRAUMA

THESE FICKLE GIFTS

Contrary to popular belief, getting shot isn't like being stabbed. There is an intense hot pain in the wound. It is like a charley horse, a muscle spasm, accompanied by compression with a molten spatula. Your entire body moves when a bullet lands: there is a lot of force in those small shells of metal. Michael Brown was shot six times out of the twelve that Ferguson police officer Darren Wilson fired.

My college town of Hackettstown fades in the shadow of large hills and opioid abuse in a lonesome plateau on New Jersey's western face. It is a far shout from the trenches of Ferguson, Missouri, where eighteen-year-old Michael Brown was shot twelve times. Each bullet was maybe 156 degrees upon release from the barrel and carried enough force to penetrate several layers of flesh and crack the bone beneath.

Six of these wounds made their mark on Michael Brown's front. One would have been the death dealer. It's unknown in what order these bullets made their mark—if the first six missed, but the last landed; if it was the first six that landed, and the last six that missed; or if it was simply a random spray.

The cruel economics of this incident does not matter to the equa-tion so much as the variables do. In these cold mathematics, every party has come to the sole agreement that Michael Brown was Black. At the beginning and end of every survivor's narrative of young Mike Brown's demise is this lasting truth: his experience, built upon the black of his Blackness, was dictated solely by the world's interpreta-tion of this unchangeable bending of light and biology.

#HandsUpDon'tShoot was the resulting hashtag.

Maybe three months later, twelve-year-old Tamir Rice sat at a Cleveland playground toying with a toy gun. Ohio winters come earlier than most throughout the country and slow the pace of any given day. It moves at the pace of frozen syrup. Car engines are stalled for hours at a time, and the average work day begins an hour earlier to compensate for the precedent. On this November day, it was no different.

Snow covers the entire city block surrounding the Cudell Recre-ation Center of Cleveland's Cuyahoga County. Tamir Rice is playing. Tamir Rice is playing in the cold.

Until roughly 3:30 p.m., when a police siren sounds across this Cuyahoga neighborhood. For this crime of Tamir's, the metals of the police car heat with a quickness. Fire rests in the belly of Cleveland's "bravest," Timothy Loehmann and Frank Garmback, and they take off across the road. The car has barely stopped momentum. A burst of thunder and Tamir's fun ends from a gunshot wound. The City of Cleveland files a claim for the family of Tamir Rice, for the cost of Rice's ambulance ride.

My sophomore year of undergrad, I took an online creative writing course at my alma mater, Centenary University (née College). It was okay. For the most part, I struggled with the material I was coming up with, as much of it dealt with trauma I wasn't experienced enough to unpack yet. My writing was largely hindered by the focus on social activism I'd swallowed whole by that time. Where my slam poetry career—as local and confined as it was—was doing great, I couldn't find a way to turn my unapologetic Blackness into a defined voice.

I no longer suffered from the fright of PTSD—at least not that I could perceive. I kept my guard up, but I didn't feel the need to be on attack. My dorm was my isolated safe space where I would tend to the necessities of this particular direction. We focused on prose—not poetry—developing a long list of short stories as a foundation to whatever aspirations we held for postgrad. I didn't hate the class so much as I was disappointed in it.

There was another girl in this class who I didn't seem to gel properly with. Her comments felt off. She never "let" me talk about "Black stuff." She had an issue with how little she understood of it. She fought me on it.

She also fought my classmate Jon on his queerness. "I'm not sure what your father's comments about your personality has to do with you being gay," she typed behind the safety of Blackboard's unofficial nonaggression pact. "Sounds like he just didn't want you acting like a girl. He sounds like a good dad."

I can't say I hated this girl.

I'll say I remembered how my grandfather's Motown documentaries always talked about "crossing over" like it was the definition of everything these talented men and women could ever do. I remember the fervor and sacrifice they threw at it. I remember how little of them actually succeeded.

I can say that this girl reflected everything I hate as an artist.

Black art is among the most fickle mistresses to house. Black artists are not captivated simply with becoming the best within their field. There is an obsession that has to be entertained: a fixation. Gifted Black children have been haunted by this disquiet phantasma since the New Negro Movement. Her name is Black Excellence.

Black excellence has no shape but is an amorphous shadow throbbing into all sorts of shapes and sizes. It twirls between the crevices of actual characteristics, and yet all Black children know what it looks like. It is being the top of your class at any costs but just shy of the best in the school district. It's coming in first for your region but coming in second during nationals—behind a white girl, no less. There isn't a simplification to what you do; there isn't doing something simply because it makes you happy.

You're catering to the elevation of your people, always.

However, sometimes I worry that Black art exists in a perpetual state of exploitation, and I cannot name a genre where such a thing doesn't exist. A timeline, in this age, is rarely composed of anything but the anguish of the many who have been owed peace for several generations and found none. And it won't stop.

Sometimes, I think of blaming the Black creators who turn their attention to this minstrel show. Writers traffic outrage and pain in a digital age for commodity: musicians who cannot find a note without gratification of a reality that only Black perspectives should soak in; directors and video giants who find a way to paint our agony in black, white, and red, but refuse to showcase the miracles between. But it's easier to blame your siblings for the symptoms of the poisoned tree. In the end, we're all fruit of circumstance, and the unsatisfying taste is environment born.

This taste is the last taint of crossing over. The forever bitterness of selling the core values of what you're doing: the very nature of its meditation on Black life and feeding it to social media for it to mill about into digestible content that appeases this momentary flash of what they want Black people to entertain. The angry Black woman with a fire and a passion for righting injustices that they were too lazy or too uncaring or too secure to want to tackle themselves; the queer Black man whose sexual agency is amplified through their own habit of self-fetishization, where the notion and context of what is done with a Black penis and what could be done with a Black penis is open for the entire following to see; the quote above a clip of a Black child's murder shared ten thousand times before the their own mother has had the opportunity to learn that they are now in mourning. The quote itself: "We've got to stop sharing images of Black pain."

This is the disgusting film surrounding this idea of "crossing over" for Black artists in this era. The idea that you can become so distant from what you originated as that you can easily find the messages at just a few keystrokes and yet the reality escapes you. And as I think back to that girl in my creative writing class, I often argue that I do not think she knew what she triggered in her comment. That, in my resistance, I was decrying her demand for more whiteness. That was never an option as a Black artist who mourned the death of Black bodies and has faced the grim truths that try to hide behind comforting lies: I was resistant to defining myself in opposition to this white girl, because my life is not according to her.

It was a lesson I wish others had the fortune of suffering.

/////////

In 2018, actress Viola Davis conducted an interview with the *New York Times* decrying her performance in the 2011 blockbuster *The Help*, based on a 2009 novel of the same name.[1] This story cataloged an aspiring journalist and southern white woman's relationship with 1960s Mississippi and its exploitation of Black maids and domestics. Despite the relative successes of the film as a champion against racism and a symbol for racial discourse, Davis reflected that the film was flawed inherently.

The truth of *The Help* is in its disservice by distorting the truths of an era defined by racism, exploitation, selective acknowledgment, and socialized trauma that were the realities of still living Black men and women. It was a zeitgeist not because it rung true to Black experiences in America, but because it made white people feel comfortable. The argument prevailing throughout the era and necessary post–Black Lives Matter was situated as a child of Toni Morrison's earlier theories on the white gaze: that we cannot be honest or engaging in Black thought if we're too concerned with making white people feel better.

How can one feel better about admitting to being the villain of a whole people's story? It's an enigma in of itself, but it's an enigma that is not the purpose of Black culture to figure out for white people or any of the non-Black cultures that populate the Earth consumed by the pestilence of anti-Blackness.

When we return to the fixation of Black Americans with exceptionalism, we often return to these gazes: these epitomes of what others expect of us, or desire of us. How we can wilt our flowers so that they allow the sun to reach other gardens. How we can strive to soar higher, further, and faster at the expense of losing our nests. We subject ourselves to the criminal enterprise of über-adequacy because inadequacy somehow means that everything everyone has ever said about us was right. And that we are undeserving of our own stories because the stories do not achieve a greater life than the ones all around us.

We strive to be gods to be equal to the mortals. As if we don't bleed, as if we don't grow tired. As if we do not sleep at 3 p.m. on a Tuesday afternoon until 6, when we finally feel the worth to face the day too late.

In 2015, April Reign curated and led the #OscarsSoWhite hashtag, which developed and led the conversation around the 2015 Academy Awards, which, for the second year in a row, failed to nominate any actors of color for all twenty slots in the best lead and best supporting actor categories. This was the first time since 1998 that anything of the sort had occurred. The outcry spread across social media at large before major media took attention to the demand for accountability from the industry that vehemently rejected notions of ostracization, bigotry, and tokenism of any kind.

Despite the many ways that this has been disproven over the course of 2010–20, the major focus from Black Hollywood in general was that the only key to true equity in the arts was to achieve through the craft and maintaining of Black excellence: specifically, the creation and maintaining of Black-owned businesses and enterprises within not only entertainment but capitalism at large.

Black excellence and Black-owned go hand in hand in any and every Black arts renaissance. It is an ouroboros of the species *Dendroaspis polylepis*—the black mamba, and not just as a cute and clearly racialized euphemism. It's poisonous as well.

Black excellence is the reason I sustained panic attacks at C grades and suffered the silence of my family when virtue alone could not guarantee a profitable future. Black-owned is where I learned that the whole point of these anxieties and silence was due to the potential profit I can garner for people who did not live in my household, solely for the fact that I could honor my family with praise from people who did not live in my household.

And, yet, I still find that comparison, birthed from the outer regions of my thought, to be callous. There is virtue in a Black community that exists in perpetual conversation with itself. It praises the crown sitting firm on its head. It preaches to the children when they find their spirits sour. The dowry at a Black woman's wedding is in the hymnals that are birthed because of Black-owned structures. Baptist faith is African faith because the churches stayed in the community. Black-owned isn't the enemy, but what capitalism does to it is and what we find in the Digital Black Arts movement as we scroll is that the enemy has made traitors of the loyal.

Black art is Black-owned. Digital Black art is not Black-owned. Twitter is owned by a conglomerate of faces, one or two of whom could possibly be Black at any given point to the extent that performing the research to verify automatically creates outdated information. Instagram, Facebook, and YouTube are much the same way. Digital Black art is hosted on these platforms. It is at the forefront of its trends as much as it is a part of our culture. However, the hands that control digital Black art are not Black and in some cases forbid the notion of catering explicitly to Blackness alone or at all.

And, just like that, the issues with Black excellence appear again. It isn't Black owned, either. It's based on a constant, never-ending comparison to people who won't understand why we're even trying in the first place. They find it cool, they enjoy the spectacle of it, but what is really understood from inside the tower of the mainstream? When the world is created to appease you, then the existence of othering is merely a departure from the status quo: it's a rock show in suburbia during a school night, and that's on a lucky day.

//////////

I fear that my people are afraid of a life made uncomfortable.

We can endure it, and there is no expectation of doing anything other than that. But I think about the many things that we have done to keep ourselves comfortable. The things we've made an art out of to put ourselves on even, soft things.

When I log onto Twitter, I come across so many Black faces petrified with spending their last days on a hard surface with the many scars to show of what they had to do to provide themselves even that. They make an idol out of capitalism where they can lay offerings at its feet and get something in return. As if finance is so fair that you can expect to be paid the worth of whatever you put into it.

In 2019, a few of those faces talked about buying back their block (from gentrification). Another few started talking about Black capitalism. Another few started talking about generational wealth. So many words for the same kind of thing. A thing that isn't a thing, but a condition.

It's a condition of hardships gone and over. It's a condition of obedience and safety. Where the fingers pointed at you have snapped and broken, and you may orient them in directions you prefer. The more fingers you orient, the greater the value of what you direct yourself.

I think about my father running the streets of Philadelphia in baggy Dickies and lanky limbs, selling to whomever has the foolhardy temptation that a Black man with a cocaine habit has their best interest in commerce. I can't estimate how many lives were ruined by his innocent fun at fondling things too far out of reach as a child, including the love of a fully present parent. I know a few dealers who say things done on the streets are done for kin. I have not known many of those men to apply that philosophy to protest and revolution. They might've benefited more in the long run from a love of community than the love of the drug trade. After all, it is evident to me that the drug business cared little for their longevity. In the end, white-collar white men profited more from numerous legalization efforts than the blue-collar drug dealers who performed its daily labor.

My mom was not far from her dreams as a rapper when she met this man. She herself was running from a fair of a life most uncomfortable; after all, Jehovah's Witnesses are not known for our capacity to be comfortable. Their relationship lasted a bit too long, my grandma thinks. But she thanks that it did, because nine months too early, and I would not be here.

My mom was addicted to the comfort of dating that a street man gave her. She was comforted by the knowledge that no one could touch her beside him unless it was him. For Black women, I can imagine the singular joy of one man's hands upon you that looks like you over dozens and dozens of others in a myriad of colors from white to Colored. My mom in grade school watched a white boy die from too many hands upon him on a schoolyard. The terror of such a thing made her loud and ardent. A rebellious spirit that lifted her tongue and became the magical voice in her work.

It's a wonder if these conditions could not be praised for such a magical voice. The fantasy most musicians work that they'll be the one in a million with gold garroting their neck and a mortgage for their glorified closets full of mink furs, real satin, and the sage-old cotton their ancestors once wove off stem and into bushels.

FRANCHESCA RAMSEY

In 2023, just after the entertainment industry danced on the tip of a needle's forehead, a TikTok influencer said it is better to have a white audience over a Black one because a Macy's campaign was not exactly selling as well as she might've hoped. She accused another prominent influencer, a young Black woman named Fannita, of relying on a marginally white audience from the comfort of her own bedroom. Black content creators did not take kindly to her saying that.

Many Black creators responded. None more seriously than Franchesca "Chescaleigh" Ramsey.

Chescaleigh (226.7k followers) was one of the first Black girls to do *it*.

It means a list of things when it comes to Black creators and the magic of dreaming up something worth enjoying, whether intellectual or base. It is different from something, because it fills up space like quality furniture that takes a community to move it in. It is something worth sharing, emulating, and remembering several years later, when you are on your back, face toward the sun-like square, picking through a timeline most didn't prefer to forget, but did in the end.

As the reactions rolled in, Fran measured the metrics of her success. There are many dimensions to such a longevity, especially as a Black creator on the internet. Namely, a relationship with the Black followers behind you.

Fran started on the internet in the ancient days of social media.

The earliest days of the internet was a wild west of HTML and Adobe Flash. AOL and Yahoo messengers were terrific for a quick talk. That's what a chatroom was, after all: a quick talk. Camera phones were less common, and images were not popularly used. In fact, most of the graphics involved on the internet were gawdy, glittery abominations like digital patches stuck to electronic boards. Usernames were something special at the time, usually close, personal, and intimate titles and nomenclatures: it was the stuff of comedy.

Growing up in the '90s, Fran didn't start accessing the internet until she had a computer. During that time, to own a computer in this era made you something of a nerd, if not also seemingly wealthy. Most people took advantage of computer cafés and library modems.

> When I was in middle school, my parents got me a computer and I had AOL instant messenger, but I was also on ICQ and I went to computer camp and learned HTML and learned how to build my own website and learned how to code. . . . I took a computer class in middle school at my school and did Mavis Beacons typing and played all these games. And I was just so fascinated by this little box's ability to communicate with us. And I think as an only child, it really spoke to me to be able to have an outlet in that way. And so while we weren't calling it social media at the time, in hindsight, we were using the internet to communicate with people and express ourselves. And so for that reason, I feel like it's just always come natural to me because it's something I've been doing for so long.[2]

During the time, "chronically online" was not a phrase for anything. No one could be online for that long for the concept of an everlasting community like that to be real.

In Fran's offline life as a middle schooler, she was isolated, like most kids are. No license. No money. A very limited worldview and, unlike this current generation, where words like "misogynoir"—coined by feminist writer, activist, and scholar Moya Bailey—were not common on social media or the internet, and if it would've been, it'd be as a cruel joke.

> And I think I was definitely not secure in my Black identity, largely because I grew up in the suburbs. I went to predominantly white schools. I was in a private Catholic school when I was in middle school. I was one of two Black students in my class. And so I think the internet gave me an opportunity to feel seen and be exposed to other types of people. And I think at the time I really needed that. I don't think I understood how much I needed it until much later in life. I was very much a sheltered kid who was very fortunate to have parents that gave me lots of opportunities and fostered those things through things like computer camp. And I went to an art school, so I was always very involved in the creative spaces, but I didn't, at the time, realize how lucky or how valuable those things were.

Fran attended Dreyfoos School of the Arts in South Florida. It's a public high school. The school infamously received major donations from Alexander W. Dreyfoos Jr. In the likeness of most of south Floridian culture, he was an avid fan of aerospace. He owned six airplanes and flew in the US Air Force in Germany. His interests in electronics and engineering and, of course, the visual arts got him the command of a forty-man photo lab that performed reconnaissance operations back when photography was among the most effective reconnaissance efforts at the time. Eventually, Dreyfoos founded a company to address color printing reproduction issues. From there, he raised a fortune.

In the '90s, Dreyfoos broke Floridian records for donations by giving $1,000,000 to Palm Beach County School of the Arts. He launched philanthropic scholarships and academic enhancements. Fran was a freshman when this donation went into effect at the high school.

Fran had many talents to contribute to the school: she played piano; she drew; she was an only child, but most importantly her inclinations toward art were not recognized as a particular priority. She'd always been loud and expressive, by her own admission; however, her mother in particular never noticed that she would take a striking interest in the arts, and it certainly wasn't a priority of education. When she auditioned for Dreyfoos, her mother assumed Fran would become a writer, taking the track in creative writing. It makes sense for most parents: writing is perceived as an intellectual art form. Sometimes, people ignore the artist's instinct inherent within writing. It is seen as something of a book smart, and, no matter the effort, it is ignored from the wider conversation.

For Black parents of a certain age, there is an allure in what is respectable. Black kids can become idle for only so long before the haint and horrors of the Greater White World are cast through them upon their child. Idleness becomes laziness, and laziness reflects a poor home life. That can't be. It becomes a grotesque misappropriation of time and duty at best. At worse, it becomes lewd fastness and thuggishness. Black girls become whores and Black boys become thugs. It is this reason why mothers in and around Philly sell their sons to militarized programs to beat the street out of them. It is why girls are kept home with chores, church, and duties as a secondary, junior wife to teach them the shame of freedom and the pride of restraints.

However, Fran was invested in acting and the visual arts. She liked that sort of thing—figuring how things ought to look, knowing where to put these things into play to tell a wider story. Visual artists and actors hold hands in the dynamic of appearances and the way it burrows through the gravel of the mind into the subconscious. The action and reaction of it all. Or, what Black folk call the "call and response." A decade later, all of these aspects would become a rainbow of experience.

"It's probably only been within the past decade that I felt really comfortable saying, 'I'm a writer. I'm a producer. I'm an actor.' I think especially as a woman and as a Black woman, there is a comfort in downplaying yourself almost as if, because the world often tells us we're not enough, it's like a preemptive measure to be like, 'Well, I act,' instead of being like, 'No, bitch, I'm an actor.'"

Fran eventually graduated and attended Miami International University of Art and Design to study, shockingly, graphic design. She originally tried acting, but found a lot involved with the craft to be pressurized.

///////////

Drama is a toxin for Black women. It both haunts the existence of most, while also being the allure of most substantive human interactions. I've seen the ways drama has become a scarlet letter for Black women of any age—rather stronger than those of promiscuity and anger. Black women who study drama face a substantially thicker wall of judgment. Beyond just the typecasting and the rigors of audition, there is a nastiness.

Hattie McDaniel was barred from the premiere of *Gone with the Wind* in Atlanta, Georgia. It was screened at a whites-only theater. At the Oscars ceremony, she sat at a segregated table with her white agent. The Hollywood hotel was entirely "whites only" at the time, but, remarkably, there was an exception made for her. She watched as her role was re-created over and over in the entertainment industry. The typecast of the sassy, strong-willed maid became refracted down a never-ending narrative, though the doors McDaniel's accomplishments opened for the talent of other Black actresses.

McDaniel's contributions to entertainment among Black thought was complicated because of the margins her roles—while expertly played—played into. While becoming the first Black actor to star in her own radio show (the comedy *Beulah*, which would later become a TV show), Hattie's show would cease broadcasting in Asia after troops complained.

The troops argued *Beulah* perpetuated negative stereotypes of Black men. Those troops declared *Beulah* portrayed Black men as lazy and conniving. This was not particularly a new depiction of Black men in American media, but Asian audiences were only experiencing American culture in glimpses through entertainment. *Beulah*'s interpretation of Black men allegedly complicated the troops' ability to do their jobs, as every Asian leader and civilian perceived Black men through these artistic liberties cosigned by one of the most well-regarded Black actors of her generation.

Black organizations like the NAACP criticized McDaniel as an artifice of stereotype. They accused her show as harming both Black actors and Black people entirely. Smears like "Uncle Tom" were loosed. McDaniel was left to defend herself from the scrutiny of the village: that most of these people criticizing her roles did so from a classist perspective. That fighting against the image of the domestics is an attempt to separate the Black elite from the everyday truths of the Black people who are most impacted by racism. Likewise, McDaniel did not publicly join civil rights protests, joined the Negro Actors Guild of America late in her career, and worked with white agents to advance her standing. She deliberately took to silence and acceptance and the status quo for her own protection against the known racism and misogyny of the industry, and the community at large declared that this, in itself, was aligning with racism.

Years later, Eartha Kitt debuted. She found great American success for her role in the original Broadway production of *The Carib Song*. She attended the Metropolitan Vocational High School (now the High School of Performing Arts). Kitt also had career-defining success overseas, such as her success in Sweden. However, unlike

McDaniel, Kitt was majorly politically active. It is not lost how Kitt's access to an outspoken nature differs from McDaniel's in the same way their skin tone does; colorism impacts more things than color, after all.

During a White House luncheon called the "Women Doers Luncheon," First Lady "Lady Bird" Johnson asked the women present, Kitt included, about the Vietnam War. Kitt wasn't there for no reason: she was a celebrity who channeled her platform into activism—perhaps the first example of a social justice influencer. It was a mistake to assume Kitt wouldn't speak her mind. Infamously, it is a mistake that anyone would expect her not to. All Black women, regardless of color, walk a fine line between the mistakes of the world and the mistakes of a powerful individual.

In a room of fifty women, Kitt raised her hand. From between pressed lips, this Black woman spoke to the world and altered her fate. "The children of America are not rebelling for no reason," she said. "They are not hippies for no reason at all. We don't have what we have on Sunset Blvd. for no reason. They are rebelling against something. There are so many things burning the people of this country, particularly mothers. They feel they are going to raise sons—and I know what it's like, and you have children of your own, Mrs. Johnson—we raise children and send them to war."[3]

A Black woman telling the truth isn't new. Ochre-brown paint exists to fill cave walls with legends of truth and historical accuracy. However, it's like a spell. Or a curse. Tituba told the truth and women swung from trees. Megan Thee Stallion told the truth and there became a punchline over podcast mics. The CIA tracked Eartha Kitt for years after she spoke at the White House luncheon. Worse, word got out that the First Lady cried: and nothing is more dangerous than a white woman's tears and the men who vow to keep them from touching barren earth.

It does not need to be said they murdered her career, or tried to. American patriotism dominates the US, but Kitt's talents were universal. Overseas she could perform freely. However, like many Black American artists who find refuge in other countries, there is a certain wound to the land built upon the blood and bones of your people rejecting you: as if they have such a right.

In 2009, comedian and Oscar-winning actress Mo'Nique appeared in *Precious: Based on the Novel "Push" by Sapphire*. The film received critical attention and awards buzz. She was asked to travel and promote the film at the Cannes Film Festival. However, Mo'Nique clarified that her contractual obligations for Lee Daniels were over. When she won the Academy Award for Best Supporting Actress, Mo'Nique stated, "I'd like to thank the Academy for showing that it can be about the performance and not the politics."[4] The period surrounding her resistance to the production company, Tyler Perry, and Oprah Winfrey was a time of scandal. The media turned her every which way but loose. She was disparaged by public opinion for not following what was expected of an actress in the spotlight. She was asked to do a lot for only $50,000—a fair rate, until one figures how much of the entertainment industry revolves around paying teams varying percentages of this total after taxes.

Most of these individuals have since apologized for their allegedly malicious behavior as revealed by Mo'Nique. Though she assured the world that as her brothers and sisters—as Black people—Mo'Nique cannot hate them; her disappointment was still palpable.

In 2019, another issue arose where Mo'Nique criticized her $500,000 pay from Netflix when compared to the multimillion-dollar deals for comedians such as Dave Chappelle, Chris Rock, Kevin Hart, and Amy Schumer. Black men were quick to disparage racism because Chappelle's and Rock's pay, and non-Black women disparaged accusations of sexism because of Amy Schumer. The intersection of it all escapes them. To many, Mo'Nique should've just accepted what she got. She sued Netflix and, in retaliation, was blackballed, again.

During a sitdown on Steve Harvey's talk show, Mo'Nique was forced to defend her integrity against a former friend. "I got labeled as difficult because I said one word and that was 'No.' Now, I said no to some very powerful people. I said no to Oprah Winfrey, Tyler Perry, Lee Daniels, and Lionsgate. And the difficulty came in when people that look like me, like Oprah, Tyler, Lee Daniels, and I gotta put my brother Steve on the list, y'all knew I wasn't wrong. And when I heard you go on the air and you said, 'My sister done burnt too many bridges, and there's nothing I can do for her now.' Steve, do you know how hurt I was?"[5]

One of the original kings of comedy, Steve Harvey, whom Mo'Nique came up with as a queen of comedy, returned that he disagreed with the way she went *about* her boycott. He called her issues "rich people problems."

Mo'Nique didn't buy that. "We are in the money game but before the money game it's the integrity game and we've lost the integrity worrying about the money."

To which Harvey returned in a powerful, authoritarian way, the king's tone—the vocals of an authoritarian, or an overseer:

"If I crumble, my children crumble, my grandchildren crumble. I cannot for the sake of my integrity stand up here and let everybody that's counting on me crumble so I can make a statement."

Mo'Nique mourned something there with her eyes red with hurt but not wet with tears. Potentially the same thing most Black women mourn when Black men fail to protect them or refuse to protect them. When they turn their sisters and daughters into sacrificial pawns for their own power. When they sell something so fundamental to their esteem.

The *Steve* show would be canceled before the end of the year. In 2024, while marketing the musical adaptation of *The Color Purple*, the well-decorated and Academy Award–nominated actor Taraji P. Henson called out the pay disparity impacting Black actors. This trend reflects pay inequities facing Black artists that is sometimes known as "the Black tax" because of how the concept thrusts itself upon Black folk no matter the industry. The term "Black tax" inflates a balloon inside the wound of the act it tries to define: to shave dimes off the dollar of Black workers is not like saying Black folk don't deserve to be paid. It is to say paying Black workers the same as white ones suggests it is equally as valuable.

A jaded population might call these issues "rich people problems" but these problems translate into serious, substantial racial disparity. How does one participate in the Hollywood machine—which controls and bends the substances of art and artists in this day and age—without the money to pay the people who maintain such a machine? Gears take oiling, levers take pulling. Calloused hands turn the wheel of the world and keep the clock tower ticking, as in Hollywood, as in society. The faces of these machinations speak for dozens who have children to feed. Their integrity keeps them alive.

Black actresses—Black women—face scrutiny universally. The smear of drama or being dramatic clings indiscriminately even when pursuing the same justices others do—whether Black or white.

//////////

In 2008, Fran kicked off her time on YouTube with some lesser-known videos on her channel. Her oldest known video is a hair how-to. Her channel was lo-fi, almost as if it were shot on a webcam. It was something like a hair channel mixed with the rapid randomness of her everyday life. She filmed other videos like "perm rods how-to," "iPhone lust," and even a response video featuring vocals in the style of Gwen Stefani.

By 2009, Fran moved to New York City with her future husband to support him as he studied law but, in the same breath, opened the opportunity for Fran to move forward.

She kept up her vlog lifestyle. One of her videos was titled "NY Vlog" followed by a few videos exploring her roots. Eventually, Fran pitched herself for the Red Carpet Reporter Contest and won—one of her first major victories.

The success put wind beneath her wings and brought her crown closer to God. Her vlog style became increasingly bolder. She filmed less hair videos and more singing videos, and what hair videos she uploaded included a lot more theatrical attention. She started doing early collaborations with other YouTubers like Soundlyawake (37k followers) and included tip videos for new YouTubers trying to build their channels and platforms. Still, her earliest work never lost an air of worry, the unsuredness that what you're doing would mean more to others than it does to you.

It's weird because I find that this is true for a lot of creative people where we are both insecure and also self-confident. It's this weird dichotomy. And I think our insecurity is tied to our need to be the center of attention and perform. We're looking for external validation because we don't have it internally. And I definitely think that that's been true for me throughout my career. And I think that that's something that, again, a lot of people struggle with, but especially as marginalized folks, this idea of imposter syndrome, it really comes from the fact that we're often told, "You don't deserve to be here," or "You should feel lucky to be here," or "You're not as good as these other people," or "You're the exception to the rule," and so at any time, it could be taken away from you, so you better fucking keep it together.

And I definitely felt that way on YouTube and at times, I still feel like that in my career where I'm like, "I know my work is good, but what's it going to take for other people to see that my work is as good as I believe it is? Wait, am I lying to myself? Am I delusional?" I'm watching all these other people hit milestones that I wish that I could achieve and I think I'm just as good as them, but maybe I'm wrong.

And so it's a constant push and pull in that regard, but I'm really thankful that I have gotten to a place in my life where more often times than not, I feel really good about the work that I'm doing. And my goal is to make work that makes me feel good. It makes other people feel seen. And as long as I do that, even if it doesn't mean I'm making X amount of dollars or winning awards or doing these things, I can feel good about it because I know that I'm making quality things and it is resonating with someone. Not everybody, but just one person is enough for me.

And then, things changed. She'd been surviving a day job in New York—like most Black artists—when her YouTube Video "Shit White Girls Say . . . to Black Girls" first went viral. It was a video recounting honestly the greatest hits of microaggressions. It was tongue-in-cheek, but the cheek had been bitten till it drew blood. The mirror it held up was polished for this singular occasion. Her content was met with mixed reviews, but springboarded a potent trend that touched almost all ends of the internet. She received criticism—accusations of racism and reverse racism and sexism and reverse sexism. She was kind in her demeanor but never shook the stigma that is inferred from—or projected onto—a Black woman's existence online. Fran, being an actor in one of the coastal cities, benefited from proximity to the famous acting spaces of New York, but with that came an expectation of controlled representation. Worse, the digital world was still a wild, wild space with not much profit to it other than the clout you could glean.

When Fran started out, she did not spar over the safety net of a partner program or a functioning payroll for creators. In fact, there was not much difference between creators and viewers then. And no one was wondering if they could execute a crossover to television.

There were no Issa Raes or Quinta Brunsons. It made every post insecure. A skittish and sensitive step into the unknown of digital entertainment that felt frightening, but necessary. As if there were no other choice but to stand out just to survive. It was an insecurity that encompassed other well-known facets of living that spread online; it was in politics too.

Fran says it was everywhere at the time. It is an instinct that, as Black people, we often have to go above and beyond to get the same level of recognition that our counterparts do not. In the oral tradition of Black culture, we say that we have to work twice as hard for half of what white America gets. However, on the internet, creators actually see it—in numbers, in sponsorships, in the speed by which YouTube and managers spring to legitimize white online entertainers as a marketing shortcut no matter what troubling, racist ideology got them their success.

Unfortunately, in the early days of YouTube, the only sure-fire path toward success was following in the footsteps of these problematic individuals. This was too far before Nathan Zed (838,000 YouTube subscribers) took over the YouTube playlist for Black History Month and pushed Black creators onto the explore page. This was before RDCWORLD1 (1.6 million Instagram followers) and Mark Phillips (2.8 million Instagram followers) injected their feel-good humor and gang-over-everything mission into the internet. This wasn't even Dormtainment's (1.11 million YouTube subscribers) Black fraternity humor. These were the people for whom drama was not a stain but an instrument for success. Too many Black creators at the time leaned into the rigid, jutting sharpness of these people—those prickly bodies that drew the blood of anyone foolish enough to bust their bubble.

The real world is often more cruel to the ambitions of Black women in a creative space. It is for this reason I can't help but look at the allure of playing the less integral role as a Black woman in the digital landscape and understand just how much pressure probably existed before there was an eventual cave. How many people understand the endurance it takes to choose one more day of hunger waiting for Net40 to take? How many people understand the imbalanced chemistry of a following whom arrive simply to see if they can break you? How many people understand how much you are only winning when you are losing?

Hattie McDaniel is remembered to have said, "Why should I complain about making $700 a week playing a maid? If I didn't, I'd be making $7 a week being one."[6]

Most pay close attention to how McDaniel shrugged off the tax upon her pay. Most pay attention to how Hattie McDaniel thrusts up a line of what she will accommodate to prevent the plight of Black women of her true social class. Not many people regard how lonely such a state would have to be. Her roles always reminding her the thin line between the Black working class she was born from and the excellence her benefactors offered her was actually a looking glass; McDaniel's flight from the life lived by many Black women further ostracizing her from the same community publicly. She stomached backlash. It was largely backlash that in the end—when people measure the lengths of power in that era—McDaniel had little control over.

One might suggest it did not matter what McDaniel had the power to impact. She was upheld as Black excellence—a pinnacle of success—as were stars like Mo'Nique and Eartha Kitt. Once success became her reality as Black woman, the drama of expectation turned criticism into theater and her reaction into sport. It is the same for every other Black woman who came after her. It is the same for Franchesca Ramsey.

//////////

Franchesca's career found its momentum when the Black Lives Matter movement activated online. Rather than ignore it, Franchesca

Ramsey aka "Chescaleigh" integrated social activism into her content while trying a break into the industry as an actor and writer. She challenged notions of systematic racism in the casual ways whiteness showed up in the public—not just in real life or behind the scenes—but within the spiritual nexus of the internet too.

In 2013, Chescaleigh began to build two-way roads with other Black women, like Crissle, who was known for her personality on Twitter back when she was "@smashedthehomie." During such times, in-between their battles against misogyny with people outside their circle, they found time to react to Beyoncé's self-titled album drop—a moment in stan history that Beyoncé herself would remind the world about a decade later. It was a small moment, but a pivotal one, that helped push the iconoclasm of the self-titled album as a trending topic. A moment that existed in the viral context of dropping an album after midnight and by the end of the hour, changing the world with a digital drop.

On that album, Beyoncé created an atmosphere where we could confront the negotiations we had to make with mainstream feminism. At the end of the day, millennials did not think feminism was interesting, or at least they didn't know what it meant. Chimamanda Adichie would eventually be framed as a TERF—a transexclusionary radical feminist—but at the moment, with Beyoncé's ekphrasis inside of her music and viral artistry, they reframed that perspective. Conversations that were permissible at the time became so much more grotesque.

This era was a turning point for many, but especially Chescaleigh. She pushed back considerably against the lives that gained most from turning Black misery into entertainment. It wasn't that she hadn't been doing this prior—however, there is an energy to what someone with celebrity and platform does that reinvigorates other interests. Perhaps it is the respect we hold for art as Black people; perhaps it is the self-gratification we feel as human beings. In any case, Chescaleigh pushed harder against the instruments of oppression moving around her.

> I'm very, very empathetic. And it's something that, early in my life, I saw as a negative thing. I felt like, "God, I'm so sensitive." I would remember being in class and we would be talking about something and I would get so passionate that I would start crying. And I always was so embarrassed by that. And I realize now that that's made me a good creative. And when Trayvon Martin happened . . . that was happening in my home state and feeling so powerless and so angry and so heartbroken for his family that I just felt like I had to do something. And that has been something that I've struggled with throughout my career, this feeling of extreme responsibility. People listen to me, people look up to me. I have an audience, I have a voice. I have to do something with it. People are dying. People's lives are in danger.
>
> And so I never thought, "Well, if I make this content, it's going to hurt my career." I never thought that way. I always thought, "I have to do something, and if I do something, maybe it could make an impact, but if I do nothing, nothing's going to happen."

I remember the early days of the online fight to legitimize Black issues on the internet. I was a part of the movement. Most of my public following came from the kind of social justice and advocacy that seasoned and aged experts currently mock as frivolous or masturbatory: most of the SJWs think-piecing eventually got PhDs in these topics for a reason.

There was a wide berth between people who talked to you because they honestly cared, and the kind of trolls who would find your location and private information and leak it to the most dangerous people involved in a conversation. Your comments would be filled with it. It made sense why the reaction to such adverse behavior is to make more content that affirmed the world you knew around you: one where racism feels your voice and presence is a threat.

"They would show up at your house," Fran says during our interview.

> [And] I'm very fortunate that I had support offline. . . . [My manager] was like, "We need to make sure that your shit is secure." We put all these certain measures in place. I mean, people have tried to hack into my website. People have contacted my family members. I have made sure to scrub all of my personal information off of the internet, and I did it early enough in my career. I got a business manager so that all my financial stuff, my stuff is secure in ways that I feel okay being accessible on the internet, and not everybody has that support and those resources, but I had a team that was like, "If you don't have these certain protective measures in place, this could be bad for us."

In 2015, when the social justice push was at its most refined, Fran launched the MTV web series *Decoded*. It was never Fran's explicit intention to become an activist on racism. However, the outspoken nature of her awareness on racism necessitated it. It was a yearning that started not in her core but from her skin—burrowing like ants through a carcass.

The drive to resist is a reaction eternal. *Decoded* reflected that.

> I started that show in 2015, there was nobody making content about race and pop culture for a brand like MTV. There were people thinking content, but the scale that we were doing was just different. And now, I mean, there's so many shows, so many podcasts.

It's really beautiful. It's really wonderful, but it's just not the same. There wasn't the support at that time, and I just have to take heart in the fact that, in some ways, my content helped pave the way, but I definitely took the slings and arrows for it.

What Ramsey created in the web series was a framework for responding to the most explicit anti-Blackness and dialogue surrounding police brutality and racialized harm. It's something I personally used in response to educators I grew up with and made the mistake of adding on social media: the ones who truly meant well, but were in the end also overworked humans.

In her 2018 book, *Well, That Escalated Quickly: Memoirs and Mistakes of an Accidental Activist*, Fran discloses the sometimes self-destructive behavior of hypervisible activism. Never discounting it, though: it has its purposes and uses. I have never been more surprised by the constant ebb and flow of the same humans who once resisted you growing into a better truth after witnessing the substance of the community in support of a progressive nomenclature. It is where I found the rose-blossomed truth that hate and anger poison the human soul in the worst way: that the antisocial is the antihuman. Always the strategist, Ramsey assures her readers with similar tips and tricks that she outlines in *Decoded* for surviving in an apathetic space when you yourself are so empathetic, that you fight to be aware.

Particularly, as a Black woman.

People might declare that Fran took a lot of this ownership of the problems on herself. That she should have just been an artist and responded to the culture of her own capital. Some say that she might have been more successful if she had. That the world can endure just one less self-righteous SJW. They do not know the endurance of Black women within a culture so apprehensive to protecting the marginalized.

The modern era of the Digital Black Arts movement acknowledges that Black women are the voice of the internet. Black creators like KHAENOTBAE (572.3K TikTok followers) declared that "the Girls who get it, get it, and the Girls that don't: don't. Obviously, you don't get it because you're not that girl: got it?"[7] and spearheaded a reaction that fuels the passion of people who think they are the center of attention. They don't need to know that such a concept spurs from the fact Black folk's entire language doesn't worry about what other people know, don't know, or care to know. It centers the self and projects it out into the world like a cone of licking flames. If one has never done that, they can never understand the energy that KHAENOTBAE had here. The innate rebellion. The nature of self-defense.

Some suggest that someone like KHAENOTBAE has little to do with the success of such a phrase because she is a Black woman. They do the same to Ramsey herself despite the longevity of her career as a Black artist since the inception of digital content as far back as 2008.

And I said this one time when [a] Keke Palmer thing was happening where I had mentioned that we've worked together, and someone was like, "Yeah, I don't believe her. She's probably just a fan." And I said, "On the internet, I know it feels like we're all on the same playground, but the reality is many of us have jobs off the internet. Many of us have communities and partners and friendships and degrees and books and all sorts of knowledge that now on the internet, you could be like, 'Well, I hypothesize . . .' To your point, 'I can use all these big words.' It doesn't mean that you actually know what you're talking about just because you have a wifi connection, a check mark, and X amount of thousands of followers."

But to many people, that offers a level of legitimacy where they then believe, "Oh, well, she knows what she's talking about. She has 200,000 followers." That don't mean shit. I know some of the most talented successful people I know have no online presence to speak of or you look them up and you're like, "God, they have no followers," but there they are doing all of these things that I wish I could accomplish in my own career because they didn't prioritize internet success. And while it can be very fulfilling and open doors for you, at the end of the day, it doesn't make you. Being popular online means nothing. And I can say that as someone that's "popular," it doesn't pay my bills.

In this era, people undermine or second-guess the experience and expertise of Black women. Worse, it can happen with those who white-knight themselves as allies. They tend to suggest that Black womanhood carries a trauma that causes those who represent it to bolster when they should state. They call for calm with their Black sisters they think are wild. They call for ease out of women they perceive as often fighting. They patronize, as patriarchy does. On one hand, we have would-be heroes who see a victim who cannot stop self-victimizing. On the other, we have villains who know a villain they can kick without losing the hero's spotlight.

There is an equal amount of unfairness between the two of them.

HER NAME IN LIGHTS

I was in a college library when Sandra Bland was pulled over at a routine traffic stop. What followed was a conversation surrounding how prevalent Black women are in the movement and artistry of our protest. It felt, at the time, that Black women did not matter in the wider scheme of police brutality, despite the statistics on the atrocity Black women face and how little men were willing to step in and help.

When Sandra Bland's movement came, there was a fight to make sure this moment stuck: that her name and her struggle could be important for all of us who cared for Black lives: who made art including this agony of losing Black life.

I find myself thinking about the loss of Sandra Bland years later, when Breonna Taylor was lynched by law enforcement attempting to turn their focus upon her partner, far after the general public lost trust in police officers. I find myself thinking about Sandra Bland's suffering behind bars, regardless of the story, the same way I worry about Brittney Griner when she was used as bargaining chips by President Biden. I remember the marketing schemes to make sure everyone knew who and what cared about Griner across the ocean when Brittney needed even one: just one person to care in front of her.

I think about all of them when I recall that Bland did not go by Sandra, her government name; she went by Sandy.

A longtime citizen of Illinois and a graduate of Prairie View A&M University, the second-oldest HBCU in the country, Sandy had been so moved by the deaths of young Black men across the country and driven to affiliate with the Black Lives Matter movement. With a degree in journalism, she resurrected taglines and the fury of the civil rights era in her hometown of Chicago.

Sandy was something of a content creator herself, an SJW: she made videos criticizing police mistreatment of African Americans under a "Sandy Speaks" series. Sandy criticized generations of ignorance and oblivious attitudes that she witnessed around her: both a declaration of exasperation and a spiritual hand held out behind her to parents and elders who might wish to avert their gaze from the movements here and now.

Sandy also reflected on her serious ideations: the sensitivity of depression and post-traumatic stress disorder. It was the proper time to do this, when people were criticizing Black attitudes to mental health and wellness of the mind outside of the church. Her friends said that she was at her best in life, contrary to the depth of some of her social video posts.

As reported by Kate Smyser for NBC 5 Chicago following Sandy Bland's suspicious death in a jail cell following a traffic stop, Bland had had frequent run-ins with the police since June 2004, mostly traffic related.

In 2004, Bland was charged by Elmhurst police with one count of retail theft. She served community service. Bland was seventeen years old.

In 2005, Bland was stopped by police in Oakbrook Terrace. The police reported she was driving too fast for conditions and operating an uninsured motor vehicle. She pled guilty. Sandy was eighteen.

In April 2009, Bland was charged with misdemeanor drug possession. This charge was dismissed.

In 2010, Bland had a misdemeanor possession charge for small amounts of marijuana and driving while intoxicated. The DWI charge was dismissed but she pled guilty to possessing marijuana in September of that same year.

In 2013, Bland was fined $200 for speeding 21–25 mph above the limit and for operating an uninsured motor vehicle. In November of that same year, Bland was arrested for an outstanding warrant and transported to the DuPage County jail.

Finally, in 2014, Bland was charged with operating an uninsured vehicle and driving with expired plates. She was convicted and fined. She still owed $2,769 in fines at the time of her death.

It was law enforcement who said that Sandy Bland killed herself in her jail cell.

As reported by Debbie Nathan in *The Nation*: she attended college under a music scholarship, participating in the grueling schedule and punishment regiments of the PVAMU marching band (the Marching Storm), while enduring epilepsy; many people regarded "Sandy" as "strong." When she died, her Sandy Speaks videos were shared en masse.

She became one of the first and most significant victims of police brutality whose voice survived her martyrdom. As the law tried to paint her as miserable, belligerent, and close to the edge, her videos and compassionate voice of forgiveness said the contrary.

Black women have often been stewards for the digital Black space and the Digital Black Arts movement entirely. They have largely been the ones to refine the space entirely. It was Black women who applied pedagogy and the internal climate of academia to what we knew of police brutality—drawing on the structure of speculative fiction and journalistic poetry—to dictate how our art became political. It was they who called out the implicit racism within the lack of diversity and story equity in the mainstream. Black women cradle the independent arts structure of the internet, keeping the urban fiction category alive with Black romance and the beauty of Black love.

It is among the many things that the trolls prey on most.

"Antagonism" is the name of the evil that Black women conquer every day. Perhaps they interpret this as a challenge: gladiators in a pit dressed in bile and red.

It was Brian Encinia who had a history of pretextual traffic stops: the idea that suspicion can give grounds to intimidation. He followed Bland for a time and pulled her over for failure to signal a lane change. A list of disagreements went down, as if there were a library of grievances that could be pulled down upon Bland. He picked everything: a cigarette, a cellphone, a tone, a pitch. After they slammed her head to the ground and threatened to tase her, Bland warned these officers that she had epilepsy. One of the officers responded, "Good."

Later, Encinia would commit perjury when he reported he had Bland removed from the vehicle to conduct further investigation. The implication could be that he ordered Bland to be removed from her vehicle in retaliation for her flippant attitude to his authority. An idea that she died for his ego—because she spoke too loudly and arrogantly, and he disagreed with such an assertion.

What most artists of our era look at when they think of this moment is a culmination of the things they worry about. That headfast

terror that comes with why we need spaces to think about intersectionality. That terror that exists in every viral moment of a Black
woman facing accosting by men who ignores the pain they can inflict
because they perceive an object built to take pain. The belief that
no one will care if the pain is not dramatic enough. Over thirty-one
thousand people tweeted #SandraBland, and two hundred thousand
people tweeted her name, but a hashtag without technique just spins
in a vacuum. It was Janelle Monae who chanted Sandra Bland's name
at the Women's March on Washington in 2017, invoking the digital
urgency of her death on such a physical, literal turf. She handed the
mic to the Mothers of the Movement. The artist Jennifer Packer
created murals to reflect the social justice fight of the time, painting
floral tributes to the beauty of life—a notable symbol considering
the shift toward a call for power for the Black lives claimed by white
supremacy, which inevitably is what brought Sandy Bland to that
prison cell. They echoed emotion beyond what lay on a flat screen.

A question hovered around everyone whenever they brought up
Trayvon Martin or Mike Brown—when we shouted their names un-
prompted: What of the women both living and resting?

What of their names?

Are men doing enough?

A lot of men said they did. They added afro-textures to their
portraits. Tory Lanez went viral "defending" a Black model on the
set of a music video. #ProtectBlackWomen became a hashtag. At
the height of the George Floyd protests, King Bach—who would
later become one of the founders of the Zeus Network—awkwardly
scrawled Sandra Bland's name on his chest under his nipple during a
video calling for an end to police brutality.

They'd been saying such things for a while, though, without ever
once really manifesting. And King Bach helped to make the Zeus
Network, which airs classics like *Joseline's Cabaret, Baddies, Baddies
East,* and *Chrisean & Blueface: Crazy in Love,* a reality TV show

exploiting an abusive relationship that ran for two seasons. It is a network that people claim exploits Black people, but mostly Black women. The creators of the network say it doesn't and in fact should be celebrated as a Black-owned broadcasting channel. I have my personal opinions.

In 2014, Cecile Emeke dropped a poem that no one can find as of the time of me writing this. Even now, it exists only in two-dimensional GIFs on Tumblr, where it first went viral. It has been so thoroughly erased that it takes me three days to relocate her identity on Tumblr from between hyper-romantic GIFs and a how-to guide for carjacking I liked for writing reasons. From there, I find out potentially why Cecile has scrubbed the internet of her most brilliant work: mostly as a reaction to everyday struggling artists mishaps and disagreements with production, compounded by her Blackness, her outspoken nature, and the dangers mixing those things involve when confronting institutions.

Her power is in her work, though—deeply invested in concerns of the diaspora of Blackness across the globe. The kind of work that finds her in the director's seat for *Insecure*, season 2.

See, Cecile Emeke, a Jamaican British feminist and filmmaker, wrote a poem discussing the misogyny of the Black men who spout support of Black women, but fail to encourage their enlightenment into actionable, realistic help for Black women's realities.

"See, he's the kind of guy that will Instagram a picture of a lion or some other African mammal, #EveryLionNeedsHisLioness/He's the type that ignores systematic and institutional obstacles and will quote reductionist, over spiritualized shit like "Stop complaining and just be the light you want to see, sis."

He's the one who talks of women as "pieces of art" to be leered at by the male gaze/Of course that's why we exist, to appease and gain your oh so great praise.

He'll talk highly about mothers, aunties, sisters and his future children that you are obliged to bear/But any other woman is eligible to be a whore, bitch, or dispensable affair. He can only see women as human if it's a family affair.

Obtaining a partner is a capitalist exchange/It's like any other purchase you obtain/His questions sound like a business meeting or campaign.

"What do you bring to the table?," "What will you do for me?"/"Can you work, cook, clean, twerk, and raise children independently?"

Or often, he speaks of you as the comical burden, a laughable drag/where your well-founded complaints are reduced to memes and hashtags. An attempt to quash legitimate reactions of self-protection and logic."[8]

The rest of the poem remains lost for as long as Emeke chooses to suppress it, but somehow the message permeates what this era has to say for Black men. And what we actually need to own.

4

Remember, you're Black before you're LGBT.

—A BLACK EXPERIENCE

GAY IN REAL LIFE

I imagine that the day Frank Ocean wrote his open letter and came out on Tumblr, his hands were shaking. His heart was light and filled with a flutter only Black boys can understand. To stand up takes so much. To stand up alone, without brothers at your side, there is so much more at stake. After all, what is there that a Black man won't do to keep his crew?

But, on the fourth of July 2020, Frank Ocean addressed what would become the elephant in the room. He was bisexual; he loved a man more than a man loved him at the time, and it was his truth. And, in a breath, Frank Ocean became the first mainstream, out bisexual Black musician in hip-hop. Early Twitter didn't know anything about safe spaces or social justice or the myths of cancel culture. It simply existed as a zeitgeist of raunchy conversation and hot takes.

I was a junior in high school transitioning into my senior year. I'd already known of my sexuality deeply for almost a decade. There was something about bisexuality that as a Black boy never perplexed me. My first assumption about the scrutiny of gayness and the reality of homophobia wasn't that anyone could be attracted to the same sex:

it was only logical. I merely assumed there was a problem with acting on something so natural, impulsive, and real.

My first kiss was on a playground slide with a boy, Cyrus. We were playing tag, just the two of us, rushing up and down a metal slide in Columbus. Cyrus's grandfather sang on the wooden bench overlooking the playground itself and behind it the deep woods. The old man sang a low song, a somber one without breaking his gaze; he sang from morning and until night, un-bemoaned by the hazards of the evening. When I eventually caught Cyrus behind the discreet curtain of monkey bars and plastic tic-tac-toe boxes, he gave me a simple peck and smiled.

I pretended to hate it, naturally. I spat on the wood chips and wiped my mouth with the back of my hand. I stared at him, and he looked down at me. He said it was a joke. "Like Bugs Bunny," he said. No one was watching us, but we still played our roles as Black men. Black men are the greatest actors known to humankind: we pretend to want so many things we don't, we pretend to avoid the things we most want to confront.

We never talked about it again, and we went on to play a lot more, until he stopped visiting his father's family in the hood. I recognize my feelings a bit more to not say that I liked the kiss, but it was an exaggeration to say that it was hated because he was a boy. I disliked the kiss because we were friends.

The low somber song filled my room as I thought of that kiss. It would be years before "Thinkin Bout You" by Frank Ocean would drop on *Channel Orange*. I was triggered. But I was also a bullet and I traveled. A wistful smoke of memory, of Black sexuality—the memory of not a kiss you enjoyed, but a kiss you were open to. I didn't like Cyrus like that. The boy in Frank's letter didn't like him like that.

It didn't change the fact that everyone involved was Black and liked boys too much to say they'd never do it.

SHADE

With the development of anyone's Black queerness comes an understanding of what conflict means as an art form. Namely, conflict sometimes feels like the entire point to social media. It's like being in a reality TV show. Within the first month of being on TikTok—which was like Vine, but if it was built by a Las Vegas casino architect—I knew that it wanted me to play the role of the villain, or at least an antihero. They wanted me to dare Pumpkin to spit in my face and then do something about it. They wanted me to challenge and be challenged forever.

I wasn't comfortable with it, but I know people who were and would be.

I know the idea: queer people are mean and nasty and we roll our necks and we pop back. There's a sass to it that is not entirely dishonest. Queer men especially tend to emulate the masculine femininity they grew up with but oversaturate it with the patriarchy they were denied all of their lives. When Steven Canals's *Pose* hit the air, a lot of viewers watching it with me as a family on the timeline were shocked that ballroom could be such a dangerous, sharp-toothed space: they compared it to competition shows like *Drag Race*.

I compared it to *Got2bReal*.

Got2bReal was a parody reality TV show made by a YouTuber named PattiLaHelle. She was a fan of soap operas, good writing, good music, the gays and the divas they loved. She could tell you about the most iconic beefs that existed in divadom—who Whitney Houston couldn't stand, who Diana Ross loathed: the fact that they were both one to the other. She could sculpt the sensitivity of the relationship between Patti LaBelle and Aretha Franklin as expertly as she could construct the intimate sisterhood between Chaka Khan and Patti LaBelle herself. She leaned into the fantasy of Beyoncé, the person, with a character of mean-spirited ego one could only ascribe to the kind of person that knew there was a time in the early 2000s when everyone not only hated Beyoncé but blamed her for Destiny's Child's first break-up. The kind of big-headed arrogance parodied on *Mad TV* at the time.

PattiLaHelle, or Andrea Lee as she was known to her friends, did not invent this concept. *ThisIsMackTV* had the first redubbing parody, and people tend to assume it was inspired by the popularity of the anime abridging trend happening at the time on YouTube. His series spotlighted the fictional beef between the singer Ciara and Beyoncé: a joke that mostly poked fun at the fact Ciara's career had entered a seeming lull while Beyoncé, with *4*, was entering a new height of her career.

ThisIsMackTV fell out of shine around the time Vine swung around, though, and Andrea, bored as can be, entered the scene. It was an instant hit as soon as it found its way around the early internet stan forums and communities. It poked equal fun at most people, while being respectful when it came to the divas and the deference they deserved. Most Black queer internet folk know a quote off the top of their heads. They typically know what "having a coconut" means. We're real "creationary" like that.

Andrea never made any money off of *Got2bReal* despite the zeitgeist it became. It was redubbed interviews from previously uploaded and released footage of the celebs. It wouldn't function as a profitable form of entertainment, unless you liked being sued. Plus, Andrea Lewis had her eyes fixed on entering the entertainment industry. Her family was extremely talented, and she looked forward to using the share of the talent that she inherited, appearing as a writer on a web series and often in association with New York's Black creatives.

Eventually, she deleted all of her videos and allowed the circle of her two-season web series to close, her legacy assured. However, her videos would survive by reuploaders who hoped to preserve her legacy and the spiritual successors to her format like *The Legend's Panel*, which more concretely situated itself among the sort of antagonistic, conflict-heavy approach of ballroom and Black queerness.

AN ODE TO LNX

NasMaraj (148.3k Twitter followers through 2022) did the most gracious thing a stan could do on SoundCloud. He uploaded roughly an hour of Nicki Minaj's verses from 2009 to 2015 cut together into an ongoing track. In under an hour and a half, Nicki's entire career and artistry was stitched into a tapestry. He didn't just include Nicki's radio hits. He included the most obscure features from her career. It was an act of fandom, a dedication to the title Nicki has bestowed upon herself as Queen of Rap—one she upheld for years.

And then, abruptly, the track vanished. It happened in the same fashion that much Black art vanished from the great servers that our time. Like smoke, because it became a general opaque. Like the many baby's teeth that have loosened, fallen, and were pinched from under our pillow. Many Black worlds became stick-figure sketches among great white pages.

NasMaraj was a Barb, short for Barbie—the claimed name for fans of rapper Nicki Minaj. I don't think it would be inaccurate to call NasMaraj the King of the Barbs at the time, but he was certainly emblematic of fandom as content and art. The Barbs were dangerous in how talented they were at this. There are some factions of Barbs who are obsessive—passionate—with their online presence. The work they put out is very similar to the aged testimonials to a body that is higher than their own found in the most famed Renaissance of Italy. It's real easy to call fandom pointless or meaningless art. That tweets and campaigns and artwork and music and fan fiction does not serve a higher quality of exaltation and satisfaction, but then I remember the Renaissance art was all about the orgasmic reflection of theology.

That ekphrasis is art about art, and that art about celebrity and media can also swallow whole this cosmology.

People perceive God as a presence so otherworldly in its ability to bestow transitional ecstasy that only works in His name are proper art. I think that we lie to ourselves every day. Both that this feeling can be limited to just God after generations of telling our people that there are people who are more important than ordinary individuals— some who are celebrities and some political icons. And that we never saw the aureoles of individuals who've proven, without a doubt, to be the substance of special. That their words have weight and send your heart fluttering. That can boil blood. For whom decisions are made in the name of, from whom actions are made to profit the many. Would the bards of Homer tell the story of Achilles in a world of pop culture, or would they regale us with someone a bit more common? Pink wig and all.

NasMaraj was a tweetdecker back when it was weird to do it. A tweetdeck was a tool for scheduling posts, but it was also a convenient way of being annoying. Annoying is an art form in an online space, a way for people to ask for attention without seeming too desperate. I've seen what trolls like to do as a desperate plea, and we'd come to find out NasMaraj had a lot to be desperate about. In 2017, NasMaraj waged war in common annoying ways, which is whatever way he could hurt the opposition to the instruments of his desperate euphoria. He twote (Twitter wrote): "Ariana Grande fans who are Muslims are such a self-drag. Your deadass 'religion' killed multiple kids for media attention."[1]

It was blatant bigotry. He doubled down on it. "Stop pretending there is no correlation between violence and Islam. The quran has several verses that say KILL!"[2]

His fellow Barbs cheered him on, and while many admonished this childish play at cruelty, it flavored the culture of young fandom. The truth is, this is just the documented hate a Barb like NasMaraj could do or has done. He has said worse, largely about female artists. He attacked bodies, he attacked sexualities. He took glee in the distraught nature he caused. He made shelters out of those who came into his mentions on that app with ferocity in their nature. He seemed to feel godlike, substituting the divinity once attributed to his idol with the divinity of online personality, where people come to know your voice, respect it, and sometimes fear it.

NasMaraj used to troll. A lot. He was a Barb, and the Barbs were an online community so used to invalidation that they scream in the name of their invalidation.

And then, one day, NasMaraj went under earth, vanishing, with his six-figure follower count—a relatively impressive metric, but overall common within queer spaces—and Lil Nas X burst out of the crust.

In reality, NasMaraj was Montero Lamar Hill. Like me—middle name Alante after the 1993 Cadillac Allante—he was named after a car: the Mitsubishi Montero. He'd been living a life that is far more similar to what young Black queer people of this age go through. He's flamboyant, but shy. He loves music deeply, but the music he loves doesn't deeply love him. He's Black and finds beauty in that—but the world dwarfs such composure and finds areas where it ought best hide. He hid in his phone, because in this world he could tailor his surroundings to his spirit. He could make things more comfortable for himself. He could live and people would live for him. A thousand miles away, people you have never touched can make you so much stronger that in the moments you might break, you will not snap.

His mother has suffered from addiction for as long as Montero can remember, and he has clung to his father and family since he's been alive. His father was a gospel singer, dedicated to the church. Most of his teen years, Montero was alone and misunderstood and too quiet to clarify. It's a reality I know well—it's a recipe to make walls out of zeroes and ones, electronic bits and cybercopy, in that flashy world of players.

To NPR, he says he started using the internet in 2012, when he was thirteen.[3] At that time, meme websites were all the rage, and when meme websites were all the rage, they were offensive and aggressive. No one survived that era without thinking joy is something you crack out of darkness. Montero's joy was the humor of the internet. The darkness was his war with being a punk: being gay, being Black, being skinny. So many strikes against him. Queerness in the Black community has only been a mortal sin since the 1970s. It was frowned upon before mostly because grown folk got married and grown folk had kids and grown folk followed the Word of God and breathed life into his word with the passion of our existence and not the rituals—though you could pantomime them well enough, but you never had to submit to them. Drag shows have been a part of the Black community for almost a century, after all—far before Big Mama's House and fat suits. But what Montero dealt with is a part of the new era of Blackness: an era where your family can forget they are supposed to love you in-between their mission of raising Good Black Boys and Girls. Where they forget to love you the same just after coming out and they do so much that these Black kids become smears on the wall where their crosses hang. In a God-fearing family, there are a lot of ways they expect you not to shame the blood so willingly spilled from your body by your kin. The blood that makes you Black, the greatest privilege in the world, will be the blood the poisons your mind—the courage you use to breathe.

Montero suffered in this atmosphere. He was depressed and downtrodden. He fled into the electric smoke rising from his phone. He became NasMaraj. Though Montero would not come out until 2019, there are still small ways that the world closes in around you and boxes you into a space. Queerness, actualized or not, is always a box outside of a warm, comfortable zone.

There are other ways that we avoid shame, like by becoming clean cut. So clean and so cut that we can only be reflected in a positive light. Almost to give our families the ability a built-in "but." Yes, he's a punk, but—he makes good money or he's very well respected or he's never been arrested or he's doing better than your child.

I built myself a legacy of buts. First, I modeled myself a sophisticant, and when I was still rendered a Black body that could be decimated after my arrest at Hiram College, I modeled myself a radical, and when I wasn't radical enough, I modeled myself a digital presence. Montero graduated high school and enrolled into the University of West Georgia for computer sciences. It tapped into one of his passions: the internet.

However, Montero had a passion for music—but he is a gay Black boy from the South entering manhood. He had to be responsible until eventually he realized it is bullshit to live for someone else. It's the privilege of the age, honestly: to come to the realization faster than generations of queer men before us. Self-acceptance comes as casually as changing your underwear or as charging your phone—both quantifiable privileges of the West. Keeping your self-acceptance, though, is different.

Montero dropped out of college in 2018 after only one year. His family disagreed with this decision, and he was forced to move in with his sister. Working at a Zaxby's shop and sleeping on a floor, he amassed a familiar sense of yawning consumption. He promoted his music online and worked around the instruments of the internet that he was used to. A lot of tweetdecking, but also the weaponization of memes. It's a tool I used before, raising money for my first novel online. Part of it was knowing how to orchestrate a viral post by relying on humor and timing. The other part was knowing that if I appear in the replies of every viral post, I might as well become a breathing advertisement for my work.

Some were annoyed. Most Black folk respected the hustle.

Montero's time was running out. His sister's hospitality was becoming exhausted. He'd have to leave pretty soon. Housing insecurity is something of a catalyst for creativity, I find. An uncertainty and panic swells inside of you. It pronounces itself in your work—that galloping is the intensity you feel in fleeing that inevitability. I had it when I first moved to New York City in the Lower East Side. It inspired me to write on *Medium*, where the most eyes could fall on my work.

It is after this intensity that Montero started writing a special song.

Montero edited a simple tune that he put together out of the spur of the moment. Something simple and catchy. Something that tapped into the "Yeehaw Agenda" folk were talking about.

Originally, the song was melancholic. The Old Town Road was not a beautiful place. I cannot say for certain if it was Montero's intentions to create something dark in the nature of this place when matched with the frightening spasm you face at such a young age: when pushed to your limits as he was: with as much darkness as he faced: with the pit inside him dangling him over a precipice as he experienced; it is a dark thing to think about. Because Montero had to change the meaning of Old Town Road to be about success. And while the initial cords hearken to bleakness, the act of changing those words to success implies that the opposite had to be true.

"Old Town Road" was about failure. A full charge into a pointless end.

Across the planet, a Dutch producer named Kiowa Roukema, otherwise known as YoungKio, was creating beats. Instrumentals that he would upload onto an online storefront. Born in Amsterdam, his connection to American music and thus Black American culture came largely through the internet.

Most importantly, in his capacity as a rising producer and musician, he learned of the profit in serving the independent artists—even as a stepping stone to larger ambitions. As it is understood, artists make a lot of money from other artists in the music industry. But, especially, you can make a lot of money from rappers. Rappers, as much as they are loath to admit it, cannot exist without their DJs. A good beat is synonymous with good lyrics—and one cannot exist without the other, if we're being honest. Anyone who has ever been cyphered at a kickback surrounded by beautiful women and half-high men knows that if the beat was actually better than what was provided, it wouldn't be such an awkward situation to endure. SoundCloud rappers aren't paying in lump sums, though, because they are largely independent. They are instead paying in dosages to lease beats for a good song. And there lies a producer's ability to profit.

If there are ten SoundCloud rappers desperate to experiment with your sound, at thirty dollars a song, you've just made three hundred dollars. Three hundred dollars can go to equipment; it can go to a meal; it can pay for another license to a song by another local artist. If you have an entire catalog of produced music collecting dust and click online, you can have any amount of money flowing in from these independent poets. SoundCloud rappers do it because they know they only need a single hit and they can do whatever they need.

One hit puts you on enough of a list to profit. The D-list might be extremely far down, but it'll come with enough of a name to be an influencer, probably. And influencers don't go hungry. Or, at least, they are good at finding angles where you can't see their stomachs at their backs. The advent of the SoundCloud artist has always been the journey of a self-made artist to maintain their self-made image. And that means not working with anyone but the grassroots of producers. The ones whose work is polished with anonymity.

YoungKio has sampled a lot of songs, but, most prominently, for a release he would eventually title "Future Type Beat" and upload for leasing, he chose a Nine Inch Nails song.[4] Some might say that this very white group would omit it from any inspiration from Blackness, but that isn't exactly true. A group born in Cleveland, Ohio—one of the Blackest cities in the Midwest—would prelude it almost as much as the birth of rock music as a genre being as Black as it is. Though we have forgotten its ancestry, it's still there. Always.

Nine Inch Nails features a banjo section on their song "34 Ghosts IV." Following the trends of SoundCloud, YoungKio puts the sample over a trap beat and leaves it alone for lease. He described it as a "throwaway beat" to *Billboard*.[5] Just something you dick around with. I've done the same on *Medium* with my short stories and essays. One day, it is leased for thirty dollars. YoungKio has thought nothing of it at all.

On SoundCloud it might not have made any motion whatsoever. But then it became a part of the Yeehaw Challenge (as coined by Bri Malandro, a social media trend where users—particularly Black users—dress up in the image of the American cowboy). And now the internet is spurred by challenges over trends. And so, with the assistance of a master tweet decker and a platform built from meme to sounds, Lil Nas X gamed the system to transform a catchy, addictive song with lyrics that are almost so dark that they turn optimistic with the right suggestion into a hit. By 2024, Black music was prepared to welcome even mainstream Black pop and hip-hop artists like Beyoncé and Shaboozey into the country genre. Few would acknowledge Lil Nas X's role in normalization.

What followed this success makes sense. *Billboard* drops his track from the country genre because it is too much of a joke to be taken seriously. Kid Fury and Crissle discuss his song on *The Read*. Major movement is summoned behind him to advocate for his song's worth among the country genre. Lil Nas X collabs with infamous one-hit wonder Billy Ray Cyrus, rapper Young Thug, and country meme in his own right Mason Ramsey in a revolving door of remixes akin to Drake's "Marvin's Room" era. Lil Nas X was forcing his one song through the gates of notoriety to manufacture a meteoric success that obscured a lot of little truths: that he suffered from crippling anxiety and doubt, that he was unsure of if he could really change his life with one track, that he was gay, that he was a Barb, that he really wasn't much of a stage performer just yet, that he was gay, that he was gay, that he was gay.

It must've been the first time in a long time Montero had to think about what it means to be a rapper and queer at the same time. It used to be a fiction. A punchline at the end of a *Boondocks* episode. Could something as masculine as hip-hop tolerate its gay members, even when they so plainly hid among one another? On a cold February in 2022, Isaiah Rashad, a perverse and masculine rapper, had two tapes leak on Twitter of him having sex with two separate groups of men. It sparked discussions not just on his sexuality but on the fact that one of the videos featured non-Black men. It was perhaps one of the more tame leaks. People not only criticized the need for the public to out this man in an industry that is so hypervigilant in its violence but to do so in such a conversation. Isaiah himself did not comment on it until his next appearance at Coachella, where he acknowledged the destruction of such an outing. Later, he'd do an interview with Joe Budden—a hip-hop misogynist of his own right who joked about his own bisexuality—where Isaiah not only admitted his newness to the sexuality spectrum, and his affinity for the title of "fluid."[6]

Rashad has ebbed and flowed from the spotlight since. Only surfacing on the app Threads to give his comic book hot takes and react to the latest news on the X-Men. There's some question on if he even considers himself queer. If we should include him among those who came out in 2022. There's a lot to be said about the down-low men who sleep with men with little to no interest in queerness as a community or lifestyle or a politic. Likewise, Isaiah does his shows and goes on tour. If we ever see him in this light, as of the writing of this line, we have not seen him step out into this light. Perhaps it's for the best. It is a harsh, boiling light that dries and withers to a crisp.

In hip-hop, queer talent does not spring to life as fully as straight talent does. It does not lend petals to the breeze to dance upon the wind. There are little places it might play, but lushness is reserved for one kind of masculinity no matter how violent or hypocritical or treacherous.

ILoveMakonnen came out as gay in 2017 to the support of many. Half of the music industry, including Drake, said they supported him. Eventually, ILoveMakonnen would have to part with Drake's label, OVO Sound. He later collaborated with Lil Peep on an album but had to leak it on his own before it came out. Trevor Bennett, Chance the Rapper's brother, came out as bisexual but has since dimmed a bit after marrying a woman and having a child. A biphobe on Twitter accuses him of doing this for publicity—I remind them that bisexuals do tend to love cis women sometimes; neither of us know him or his truth and we end the conversation on a deadlock. Later, Tyler the Creator comes out as gay on his album *Flower Boy*. However, he is a troll, and I do not take him half as seriously as I do Lil Nas X. Because to be Lil Nas X, savvy in his social media game and savvy with how he frames himself and his work, you have the consequences to being yourself.

Lil Nas X struggled for a BET Awards nomination from the moment he officially came out—simultaneously as gay, but also as Nas-Maraj and, thus, a Barb. He likened the decision to being afraid the industry would find out he is gay. Not like people couldn't tell, but it still strained the fabric of Lil Nas X's credibility. With that fear came an innate terror of confirming he was a Barb or one of such a level that he ran a tweetdeck in the name of his face.

There might be some straight Barbs in the world, but it is not the assumption being given to dancers or the directors of the creative endeavors that if a man calls himself a Barb, that you are to see him in a straight line of sight.

Lil Nas X continued dodging the allegations when he dropped his EP 7. One of Lil Nas X's most silent, yet effective supporters was Isaiah Rickland (2,011 TikTok followers), someone who'd become a part of one of the largest social media scandals in Twitter's history when he impersonated a Black woman on the viral and popular Twitter account Emoblackthot (157.3k Twitter followers). Through the grapevine, we hear that they've been dating, but no one corroborates this. Most figure the soft unclenching of this pairing was ruined one October morning when Emoblackthot revealed themself after years of tweetdecking mental health social posts and asking other Black women about their periods. Emoblackthot was in a group chat with me and a number of other Black writers.

He never spoke about himself or on Lil Nas X, but he did speak that he did not want to open or engage their DMs because many people add them to their group chats randomly and he felt awkward about leaving so he just ignored all groups flatly. They genuinely seemed to be an even-tempered person online and supportive of Lil Nas X's sound. Eventually, when Emoblackthot's bubble burst, he disappeared from the public eye. Of course, on an app like TikTok, he has tried to return. He has made periodic posts for users to unclench their jaws. He has given mental health and wellness checks online. But there are limits to what desires can benefit you on an app designed to sniff out inauthenticity.

Lil Nas X and this boy don't seem to be a proper match. Not on paper. But sometimes queer dating is never about finding proper matches. It's just the hunt for another Black sock, whether it is also cashmere or merely just wool. Perhaps this is why queer people find such hard-earned communities online. Because we are so used to seeing the alike in the different. In ignoring the rough textures and smoothing them even. You can walk on two legs like that and no one will ever notice anything. In the end, we might not know the real Montero too. The real Montero isn't a troll and he isn't a superstar. The real Montero either yearns and aches and hunts for others to get him in that way those who are Black and those who are Queer salve in all sorts of manners. And, just like many of those people, they do not sometimes think too deeply about the matters of a proper match and being seen and the circumstances of how they got here and who got hurt along the way. They worry about how fast the next check is, so they can continue on never thinking again.

I don't doubt the honest feeling that the world owes us that much sympathy.

SEE TO BE

As a little bird-chested six-year-old, I never knew Black men to be writers. Imagine me, knock-kneed with a chilly-bowl and a soft part cleaving my hairline like a righteous blade, cut from the mechanism of my eternal joy: the written word. I imagine you reading this. I imagine the fantasy most folk cast me in inside a classroom or campus or behind a shining screen, where the idea of my face is an approximation of photos I've shared.

"He probably grew up wanting to write. He probably clutched a journal to his breast everywhere he went. He probably ate up words like Saturday morning Fruit Loops and this is where a writer is incubated and birthed."

Y'all would be wrong. I failed every spelling test; I thought grammar was some shit white people made up to make me sound stupid; and we were a Cinnamon Toast Crunch kind of family. And books you understood were made by white people with white names like Seuss or Dahl or Carle.

I was as distant to a book as I was to the appetite of a dream more complicated than what my body could do today.

That is not to say I was a stranger to the written word. My grandfather, Robert, kept a towering library with the encyclopedia and manuals with thick brown-leather borders and gold trim on the letters. There were novels too—including a flimsy paperback novelization of *The Wiz*, with the bleached colors and bent corners. After school,

I'd run home and kick off shoes and peel off socks and climb that tall wooden levels as high as I could to pick a book and bring them down.

I'd trace the letters as if I could read them real well: hitting hitches when a syllable pushed pass the limits of a six-year-old Black boy from underserved schooling and latchkey programs. When those hard walls came, I'd surrender in my ignorance and step away. When I tell my shiny-brown-faced niece this, she frowns.

"Why ain't you just google it like you tell me?" She smiles with her loose teeth, oblivious to the ways I push her to use the tools denied of me. To not take them for granted. My grandfather never wanted me to take the internet for granted. He plugged me into the electricity of infinity.

But the internet had pictures. And the best of books did not. And if they did, in the books with shiny plastic wrappers protecting the board from the exposed elements of a world more violent to them than it is to a young Black frame, they were in black and white. And the faces pale, like spectacular ghouls caught in casual winter. And, at six years old, book in hand and a fading attention span to hold, I knew one thing:

Black faces don't turn ghost when a camera goes flash.

Because I knew Black faces filmed real well. We filmed best in performance.

My mom took me to see the UniverSoul Circus early in my youth, because seeing Black people on a stage, she thought, was the most important tradition of any child. It teaches something fundamental, she thought. That you could command attention. That you could be worthy of something. That there is little more respected by our folk than someone with the skill to command a live audience.

See, the UniverSoul Circus is not like other circuses. Their clowns are cool. They keep the makeup to a minimum, always sure to show that bronze-brown skin peeking from beneath the soft touch. They wear sneakers or tap shoes—something they can dance in. And chile, they got the steps. They kick, spin, and step. Not just funky jesters—they perform with a vigor and mastery of Black dance that speaks to the hum in the red hot blood. About them are women—scantily but colorfully clad. I don't think there is ever a moment on that stage—with zebras and dancers in white and Black acrobats and Black musicians—where a soul is alone. Not that they cannot hold their own, but they are masters among masters among their people. Showing out and showing off.

Their tricks are spectacular. They play soul music. The ringmaster thrusts his hips to a jazz horn every half measure and then explodes at a rowdy crowd mid-thrust to a thousand Black adults wiping tears from their eyes.

Not like white circuses, an affair I always found sad. Their clowns are terrifying. White men caking themselves in white-out paint and colored Afros like snow cones on a hot summer day. Their clowns are the reason why, on an August weeknight, folk sparked threads asking the question of if clowns are a kind of minstrelsy—because anything that makes this many Black folk uncomfortable has to be rooted in racism.

The UniverSoul Circus was a baptism of the blood. I held it in such dynamic regard that when my mother told me the reason my daddy would not be coming to visit me this summer while my sister, Alexis, got to see her daddy for two weeks and Corvetta got to see her daddy over a weekend, was because he was touring in that same circus.

I remember smiling and nodding, settled. Because what can a single son's desires matter to such a higher calling. The calling of a Black man to perform. To create. To inspire.

I'd been baptized in smaller rituals before, as is expected of a Black American child. At seven, in the bleeding streets of West Philadelphia, at a house on a block that dodged bloody violence by the sacred understanding that kin and kids were here (a sacrament with an expiration date), I glanced over a metal rail painted black that chipped every summer to expose ribs of reddening rust. I smelled the aluminum and bitter of turned lead paint.

There were a crowd of Black men in a crowd dressed all in black so they became shadows spackled on my memory. Black like the men who broke the sacrament a summer prior under the oblong loophole that they were not busting shots on our block, but at a small patch of green across the street; I saw a man's head split like a melon. I saw him fall. I know he died and I knew this was not that.

They had the same intensity. Of a gunfight between Black sons. The air did not smell like the violent burning, but I conjured it. The crowd was frenzied, but so controlled that a small sacred loop set in the middle. Two men dotted that space. They invaded one another like carrions raking one another with pointed, terrifying claws.

UniverSoul Circus was big lights, big energy, and big brown faces. Thick was seasoned boiled peanuts and the wild spice of Black bodies so close. It was what it meant to be on stage. And, still, Black folk in the crowds were never of one mind.

A girl of around four with a neon beret that clacks loud and glows in the dark cries when the Black clown gets a bit too close. She pinches her ears with the cuff of her wrists when the singers cut loose their craft. She hates the caramelized nut of the boiled peanuts.

I say this because I never realized that the digital world would be such a circus. A cacophony of performances. And I mean that with my full chest, with every crook of joy and jeopardy.

Perhaps it is the intention of being online to always react or give someone something to react to. Every sense can be appealed. You can taste the outrage on the screen. You can smell the fear in the blood of a victim.

5

"We gotta work twice as hard for half of what they got"
or "Ain't that bout a bitch?"

—SOMEONE'S BLACK DADDY

STILL WORKING

My chosen father, Van Collins, was an alcoholic. I often find myself begging people not to confide their own stories of family trauma when I say this: I loved my dad better drunk. He was vibrant and charismatic when drunk, even when his kidneys, corrupted, gave him the musk of married 40-ounce beers and Newport 100s. He was an irritated stoic who hated losing even to five-year-olds, and I loved him and he spent so much time alone that even when I became better than him at the games men played with fathers, I still let him win.

Van taught me to accept the fireworks before the parade, the spray of sulfur that would not kill me from allergy before that flashbang— the loudest thing that could not be called "ghetto." He taught me that celebration is the reward to a job well done, not the acknowledgment that what you did was worth something, anything, everything. It was a perfect lesson for the hellscape of freelancing as a Black artist.

My people on the internet celebrate as often as we grieve or complain. We celebrate little moments and little things, captured in a portrait or in a caption with words sing-song without the spellwork of our voice. The beauty is sometimes conveyed in capitals. The thrill is sometimes in the tone. A diss to the enemy on the opposing team that ricochets into larger and larger quote retweets; the sordid GIF when a Black woman gets her flowers at an award show; showing out during prom season; the gluttony of scholarship as the college acceptance letters roll in; Four exclamation marks at the tail end of GOOAAAAAALLLL!!!!

We celebrate so boldly in public for every moment we couldn't. Victories do not come as easy as we have expected. What we win and why we won it and what we get when we really win aren't always the same thing. Angela Bassett is an undisputed Black legend in every acting metric.

It was in 1991, four years before my birth, when Bassett broke into Black America's hearts in *Boyz N the Hood* as Reva Devereaux, a single Black mother raising a young Black boy into a Black man and struggling. The struggle with a deep-seated rage, a frustration and a wrath of pillowing poisonous smog with his environment, and with his people and with the unfairness of his royal crown's tilt when he stands too fast, tall, and proud. In the end, Bassett keeps her son alive: a shocking victory for a Black mother.

Bassett claimed no awards for her work.

It was in 1992 when Bassett became Betty Shabazz, the prolific wife of Chicago Red, Malcolm X himself. Her portrayal moved along silk-thin webbing of Black womanhood. Bassett was the wife that Malcolm X truly allowed himself to love, to worship, his perfect partner and spiritual/intellectual equal. In the tradition of Islam, her hair was bundled in cloth and dower. Her eyes, glazed with hope in Malcolm's coming tragedy, reflected a saint who'd still his tempest. When he was rage, she was unphased. When he was peace, she was tranquility. When he lost his life on stage, she became the diligence that kept his legacy alight.

Bassett took home an Image Award for Outstanding Supporting Actress in a Motion Picture: the Black award. From the Chicago Film Association, she took home nothing but a nomination for Most Promising Actress.

It was in 1993 when Bassett became Tina Turner and showed us the depths of pain a survivor can hold in their vessel; she showed us the silver-lined sublime when survivor becomes liberator. A face built to chisel and mold grief into liberation and then the release to joy, explosive like the peak of the mountain of a laugh. That capital H in a Ha just before you dive off the highest point and fall to the plummet. As Tina Turner, her hair was many things—wild and free, shocked into submission, tangled, matted, truthful, and full of fable. She was her lover's envy. She was his greatest triumph. She was his greatest enemy. She was his salvation. She was his sudden collapse into Dante's flame-struck circles. Bassett became the Queen of Rock 'n' Roll and ruled the hearts of Black Hollywood.

Bassett claimed no award that year. Her costar, Laurence Fishburne, also took home nothing that year. It was the second film with two African American stars to be nominated in both the Best Actor and Best Actress categories. The first was 1972's *Sounder* with Paul Winfield and the legendary Cicely Tyson—who also never received an Oscar, but did receive an Academy Honorary Award in 2018. How does that work, exactly? Racism, some cry . . .

I say this because an accolade is as contentious to the Black community as chitlins. Chitlins is the food of our ancestors. A long rich history behind it, so many ways to prepare it. You can spritz it with vinegar. You can be like my daddy and douse it in hot sauce. You can sauté it with butter and garlic. You can do a lot of things.

And you're still eating something days ago that was marinating pig shit. Still, if you hungry, chicken shit marinade can be a whole lot of things. Black artists have never had our due in the awards season.

With the Academy Awards, we know they've played in our face with a lot of things. I was there on my mama's sofa that could fold into a futon when Halle Berry took home the award for Best Actress in 2002. My momma was two feet away from me applauding but muttering about how Halle had to fuck old-ass Billy Bob Thornton to get the Oscar. I don't agree with this sentiment as much, but I have been accused of finding beauty in art that depicts the capacity of redemption within our society for villains, the grotesque and the unforgivable, which is what *Monster's Ball* is really all about.

IF WE CAN'T BE GAY HERE, WHERE CAN WE BE GAY?

Black sexuality might have to sing itself loudly in the Digital Black Arts movement to be heard over the booing crowd. It's nothing new. Sexuality as the primal flame of revolution and radical storytelling has always been resisted in one way or another.

In 1920s Harlem, Black queer folk were the fire in the sultry-salted sex of the deep New York night. Jazz is gay. Poetry is gay. A cigarette over a glass of whiskey at a single circular table is gayest. And yet we forget the loud queerness of Harlem because of the conservative movements sweeping it under the rug.

Freedom is never spelled by those who are afraid to be as open as they possibly can. When I think of Countee Cullen's heritage pondering:

"What is Africa to me?"[1]

I find a man questioning not just Africa's vision. I find a man questioning so many aspects of a Negro's reality. Negrotude incarnate. Questioning masculinity and femininity. Questioning his sexuality through wild, wet, and carnal exploration. I see explosions of passionate colors—deep blues, indigos, and burgundies. The sweet cinnamon swirl of coffee on a midnight wind. Butt fucking and thigh slapping morning, noon, and night.

When I think of my Blackness and my Black art today, I remember how often I fall in lust with singers. His voice wasn't too good.

The first time was the earliest eve of my bisexuality in high school. It was 2012 and he was too old for me, and I did remember that at the earliest points in our relationship. But I hadn't read James Baldwin and I hadn't realized the impact of the Harlem Renaissance awakening the backwoods Black queerness that is as ancient as consent between unfreed Black folk. I just knew the heresy of the present day, sans the arts. A muted living without the bombastic colors of the carnelian browns you don't find in the Crayola box. It was a world without the swish of the hip or slender of the wrist. It had no sing-song to the voice like every word is an exalted gospel—what a joy to be alive, let me speak with the same praise.

A world without queerness. A world without art. In such places, not much is worth breathing in.

No wonder a Black boy falls into the colors of any old boy's eyes, the distance between him and me where even if you know you won't find yourself, you can find something to tell your friends about.

He was a Black artist, too, with round lips, a round head, and a collection of snapbacks that put my dad's collection to embarrassment. His weekends were dreams of road trips to Cleveland for this audition or that. He was an actor. He was a singer. Sometimes, he was a dancer. He ran through friends like he ran track—saying he was going places as others ran ahead in a happy new group. Fortunately, there's always someone new starting the race where the boy running in last place is running ahead of you. He borrowed the camcorders of local whiteboys from the Riverbend neighborhoods in Columbus to capture the odd auditions. If he didn't get the part, he backed those videos up on YouTube. Someone would pay attention. Someone will give him a boost.

In this era, YouTube had just become profitable and then fell out of profit. Chescaleigh smiled on camera with a head full of locs. GloZell Green (1 million followers) did the cinnamon challenge, choking back a fistful of cinnamon from a wide ladle, wearing a dress and bangles the color of sweetgrass and the neon vomit of Nickelodeon slime. When she gagged up a cloud of that same cinnamon, when that cinnamon coated her throat and choked out moisture, when her throat exploded with fissures of force and she fought back the tug of death and clung neon acrylics into the thin skin of life's illusion—she did so with a thought about the algorithm's attention.

Of having something to show that looked familiar to a job well done. In a few years, GloZell would fall on hard times after the limelight of YouTube's golden era, and we mourned for her while others celebrated brand deals and rising media contracts.

In Ohio, we did nothing of the sort.

DAZZLED WITH DESIRE

Toni Morrison exposed me to the interior pain of desire. That wound that stabs outside with barbed thorns so, when lodged, it'll stab you from the inside out. It is the goal of the master narrative, she puts it. The lie told again and again until it becomes reality. It says you are ugly: nasty for this and nastier for that. That skin as cold as Black. That hair as coarse as raven-flock. Lips pronounced to kiss. Noses like rocky mountains and heaping blocks of hay.

In the great canon of desire, upheld by the master narrative, Black folk are not there. Of course, there are little footnotes, as expected for a people on the margins. However, think of the Blackest person you know. Cold and broad. Don't alter them, see them without makeup. See them without all the little instruments of exceptions that we master from childhood with a hot comb, relaxer, wig, or brush. See this Black person in their natural beauty.

Would the internet call them beautiful? Would the internet fawn over them? Might the internet seek their humility when they are unkind or simply jaded or flippant with their bravado?

Think they won't be. I've seen it. They've seen it. They do not need your sympathy, because even the sympathy has the sacrilegious stain. That nasty grit and grime caking the nailbeds of this culture.

I wonder what they would call that video of Ari Lennox, the singer, in her fur coat and minidress, her hair pulled into a tight bun high like Cindy Lou Who surrounded by Black faces—like Guapdad 400 with a drink in his hand—jigging around her, aiming their shining mirrors with the flash on, illuminating every inch of brown skin as she sings "BMO." It is, to me, such an iconic portrait of beauty. It is sexy; it is like seeing lightning striking close to home. It's like the shimmering of the windowpane with your hand against the glass. It is like fingerpads dancing against knuckles then fingers then knotting into clasped fists in a dimly lit movie theater with blown-out speakers.

I have been guilty of chasing popularity for beauty when online.

I have wanted to be worshipped for that sort of thing, even in the trenches of masculine performance. I know many dark-skinned boys who'd want that sort of thing. To be seen as beautiful. The sons who've dodged the sun have a thirst for the spotlight as any cave dweller. The daylight is warm on cold skin. It makes you smile; it makes you seen.

I have been hit on, of course, but not because I was desired. You can tell the difference. When you are desired, you need not speak. In fact, the world prefers you don't. The less they know your voice the better. On the apps, you can get things for being so beautiful. Doors swing open and you can step out of the sun and into the cold at your leisure. Influencers got real good at picking apart which of the two they can do.

But, again, there are rules to who gets to do this. You have to be this, not that. That, not this. You can be Black, but—as we said—there always a but.

I do not have enough buts. I'll probably never be desired. You learn to admit it to yourself as you struggle to rise to the surface of the social networking game. People don't engage you as much if you don't have something poignant to say. Perhaps if you became the sort with something outlandish to say—not necessarily important, just full of that violent oxymoron of humor. You can get that quick dopamine high of virality. You can be seen by your favs or your fav's favs. You can get in the fight with someone you've been jealous of for months or someone your fingers have hovered over the gateway of following. You can feel like there's a point to it all even though in about a week, you'll barely remember what was so important about what you spread in this moment. Perhaps you'll anger someone who will bereft you in a language you do not speak, and Google will offer a translation for a new slur for your Black ass. You'll plumb how you are hated for a moment. You'll move on a little less willing to do this again. Or perhaps you will. . . . Self-harm holds its own dopamine hit, in the libido of the senseless.

Desirability means these agonies go a bit differently. That the doors open just a bit wider.

I knew I was undesirable when I debated my friend on the public timeline in 2021. I'd seen how this goes before. In the earliest moments of the #BLM hashtag, the social justice warriordom was only a spring chicken. Tumblr crumbled and we came over in exodus. Black Twitter had been such a nascent thing. Twitter was just the place where Rihanna called Karreuche Tran a rice cake and told Teyana Taylor she was a "broke bitch" and that Teyana was "Screaming in an empty room! #dontfeedtheanimals." It was a place for mess, and mess could be entertaining when you are wonderful to look at.

But the Tumblr girls were here. And they had a new name scratched from the rapid schisms on that app. Social Justice Warriors. The kind of people who were self-righteous, but self-righteous for a cause. It wasn't just PC, because political correctness was not even what was the appeal of these people. After all, being correct comes second to being just.

At the time, there were plenty of Black queer people I've come to expect to see anytime an issue cropped up. They had nasty things to say about anything, but they were always beautiful. Many of them were light skinned, with eyes closer to carnelian rock than carrowed black pearls. They read people for anything if they felt slighted. Fatness. Health diagnosis. HIV+. Sex work.

I've learned most of the ways being dark skinned was not welcome in the queer space from just opening an app. I've learned many of the ideas of what might happen in ballroom from these people who borrowed its dressing without any idea of its culture. I've learned I am not beautiful, but I had not learned what it meant to be undesirable until I debated my friend, who was.

Our conversation started as it often did: pointlessly. Most of the internet had only just returned to one of the greatest shows in history—*Avatar the Last Airbender*—at the earliest crust of the global pandemic in 2020. It was supposed to be good fun, is what I remember. A nice way of passing time until a new hot topic with hotter content drops.

My friend said: Korra from the *Legend of Korra*, the sequel of *Avatar the Last Airbender*, was a horrible Avatar.

I said: If Korra is so terrible, Aang is sinisterly awful at his job.

He argued that Korra was getting knocked around the room and that she was too hotheaded to function.

I argued that Aang was a manipulative bald-headed Caillou whose one claim to fame was causing a genocide and still being so selfish as to feel entitled to his spiritual enlightenment as if murder cheapens one person forever. It's a dumb argument. I've hated it as an idea ever since Batman made the claim and ruined superhero comics forever. I ramble often that Haitian revolutionaries were not cheapening themselves when slaughtering slave owners. I ramble often that any oppressed groups' unwillingness to resort to killing their oppressors is directly correlated to their own compassionate morals and not the measure of their humanity. It is my habit to globalize many things, because I think hard and often about why I feel a way about a topic and to what lengths I am willing to go over where that emotion is tied to the fibers of my character: to avoid bias, to realize what biases I am unwilling to compromise, to allow myself the privilege of joy every once in a while.

But my friend is not as rigid an abolitionist as I am, with deep feelings on cause and effect that limit my daily life. So, we debate about cartoons.

But to stand opposite a beautiful person as a creator when they are also creating for an audience hungry for their attention is to excite danger. They acted on it.

We've both deleted and blocked a good sum of what happened next.

One of my friend's followers called me a "roach": something he would never agree with. Being called a roach as a dark-skinned person has several implicit damages that I can register in my internal climate. Black like thick Miami rain clouds. Dirty like the blacktop of a Queens playground. Shiny like oil from black seed.

I don't know if my friend blocked this person back and I believe he did and would, but this situation clung between us for how it made me feel overshadowed by my looks. It wasn't the first time I've wrestled the beast of the eye, but I wasn't an out queer man then. I wasn't constantly wrestling with the insinuation of sharing a space with a friend so much more conventionally desirable. Not attractive—my mother told me she didn't birth ugly babies, and I believed her. And it wasn't about things I *know*. I wasn't wrong because I wasn't pretty. Something about this new notion hurt me deeply: to know that I could have the one thing that I could rely on—knowledge—diminished by what I looked like by people who looked like me. But desire is not about what I know about myself, but the rules of the game. The rules said I had to serve desire if I wanted to share space with it and if I was not of service, I am taking up space, eating up resources, and being a nuisance.

A roach does these things too. I see the comparison in the slur.

//////////

Years later, the desire created its own market. Another of my friends joined it: he became a model for OnlyFans. It's a website that popped up out of the wilds. It isn't the oldest website for people to share videos and—honestly—pornographic content, but it is perhaps the easiest to use. Most sex workers (pornographic models and the like) used Just for Fans once upon a time, and still do, but over the quarantine it allowed people to make use of lo-fi, DIY setups for sharing content. And you didn't have to be that good, if you set the price low enough. You could steadily increase the price as you went and there was lucrativity to it. Better, less and less people were judged for engaging sex in this way. Most influencers jumped ship. They lost out on the slower, heavier paychecks that could accrue over a career and focused on the rapid success they found on OnlyFans. Whatever their audiences wanted to see, they could provide for clout and capital, and they made a *lot* of money. There was a lot of conversation regarding what was a "real" sex worker and what wasn't. A man I interviewed did not see himself as a sex worker: just someone who liked his nudes and knew people would pay for it, even if they would get demanding and possessive.

"Real" sex workers didn't like it. They said that things like Only-Fans both trivialized the things that sex workers do and have done, while also overinflating the market. People had to get creative to sustain the attention economy that would reward them with more and more work.

Eventually, an art form was cultivated and in spaces with the most money—like queer men—there became communities with its bigger players. Once outside opened back up, these people co-opted the power and privilege of celebrity. Queer men have always made porn actors into pseudo-celebrity: the male gaze will always be the male gaze, but this shifted things a lot more in the favor of independent sex workers. The stiff competition meant that people—especially escorts—had to create content that appeased not only Black consumers but anyone who was willing to shell out money in support of their creators. "Serious" models started traveling to exotic locations or curating settings to make the money worthwhile. There wasn't much need for a "day job" after this when people were making somewhere in the upper $6,000s a month for their content. And with audiences like that, it also bestowed influencer status onto people. Nothing official enough for brand deals with companies that had a public anti–sex work stance but definitely enough for party-lovers.

What used to only be opportunity for go-go dancers, drag queens, and strippers during Pride Month and beyond became an entire sector of entertainers whose one job was, as a former friend put it, to be pretty. And for men, that had a lot of requirements that had to be met, from having a personal trainer to cultivating a social media following that operated like a cult.

In Black queer spaces, ballroom enabled a lot more traction and fandom. Shows like *Pose* and *Legendary* introduced the culture and magnified niche interest in groups and Black queer spaces where this performance can be done: a chance to run into OnlyFans models being normal and having fun? Of course, promoters and owners started paying people to host and "perform." In New York, this typically went down at circuit parties or the few Black queer-owned bars in the city like Club Lambda. Micah Martinez started Deviant events, a circuit party for Black and Brown queer people.

Each of these places had its superstars and enough money flowing through it.

There is no official name for this industry that my friends started flowing into. I started calling it the "Pleasure Industry." It was a near-perfect recreation of the Red Lantern district of Tokyo and the geisha who populated it. There was escorting, hosting, collaborating, and more, but for the most part everyone received opportunities based on the fantasy they could promote—their position within desire. They refined the techniques outside of sex. In fact, most models in the pleasure industry were not *explicitly* good at sex work. Some didn't escort at all and had strict rules on who they slept with for content and why.

Opportunities typically aligned with the longevity they felt within the career path. Like geisha, it was the hope of some to fully abandon OnlyFans and content creation for a job that can meet their financial needs without the tainting of their sexuality. See, while most people who engaged in this industry did in fact enjoy sex, capitalism has a way of putrefying whatever thing you love. When your body is involved with this, the kind of unhealthy tactics manifest in other areas. Many OnlyFans creators—surrounded by alcohol and hard drugs—quickly developed addictions. Others endured untreated mental illness, as even with the money they made, it is not exactly a career with terrific health insurance packages (despite many having up-to-date sexual health). And then there were the dramatics and the impact on their social lives: many sex workers in these spaces had very public explosions of some kind that they had to navigate around. Some orchestrated horrible comments and hot takes—from fat phobia to colorism to bottom shaming. Others enjoyed inventing a new type of person they were better than. There was also the prevalence of race play—the sexualization of racism—among groups of Black creators with a large white audience and white creators with, sadly, large Black audiences. They knew exactly what would pay their bills.

Most models, known for their desirability, their beauty and bodies, found their spirits irrevocably damaged from the chase of controversy and diminishing returns on their personhood. Many of them didn't realize the trap until it was too late. Seasoned sex workers, the ones who recognized what power looked like and what it didn't, tried to warn them: particularly when their *first* politician or rich man got involved with their content.

There is no such thing as fast money. There is no such thing as being loved for beauty alone.

Because, even with their following, many became too afraid to let go of what was hurting them at the center of desire.

2019

I became romantically entwined with the celebration of the job well done.

Independent work is often a road of sharp rocks and cantankerous detours. And warning, for there are bandits along the way and many miles before true rest or satisfaction. A friend often jokes that despite my relative popularity and stable following that I have the worst choice in collaborations. While simultaneously, my rise in August 2018 was almost meteoric and attributed to working with the right people.

In that year following August, I did not make much money. I moved back in with my grandmother and let myself become a wash-out. The darkness swallowed me, and I proceeded to wait for winter 2019, when I could move to a suitable MFA program and work diligently as a slave to the American academic standard.

You ask yourself a lot of pointed questions when you're going for a graduate program. Those questions are sharp enough to draw blood.

The wounds might get infected if you drag a little too long between asking questions and doing something with that information.

I saw myself going to an HBCU for one reason or another. Historically Black colleges and universities have everything to offer to a young Black mind. Ta-Nehisi Coates walked into the halls of Howard and found knowledge's stiff kernel rested in flotsam within his chest swallowing heaps of salt and rushing sudsy water until it rested bitter and fertile on a sandback, ready to burst into an orchid. When he went to school, social media was chat rooms and forums, little low-res and uncool things that preoccupied time rather than stole it. I once likened college as a Black man to an illegal kind of living. Every step, a violent uphill.

Instead, I went to Hiram College, where the Wi-Fi was so spotty that if you sent a tweet in the morning, it might post by the end of classes at night. So spotty that my roommate's gaming rig took up most of the broadband for our dorm. So spotty that context arrives hours after offense has been taken. Bad things happened on that campus. I was arrested, sadly. I was charged for causing a false alarm for a tweet that, while poorly timed, coordinated the language of where I grew up and with whom I found myself growing with—Blackness, and the myriad languages we speak while speaking English. I never thought about translating this language, like I do not think Ta-Nehisi Coates thought about translating his own background while hopping the libraries at this mecca where most people were not Black in a new way, but Black in a way that they could put names to the people who hurt their families ancestrally.

During this time, Kenny Knox had been building his platform from the ground up. He'd been struggling after growing six thousand followers organically. The internet wasn't a strange place: Kenny'd been surfing social media like MySpace when he was way too young to be doing such things. But he was preparing for a certain kind of lifestyle.

See, Kenny once told his class that he would grow up to be a comedian, and some little dickhead laughed at him.

Kenny has had someone to prove wrong ever since.

Vine in those early days had its own icons and stars. King Bach was one of the most popular creators on the app. His content was satire. At this point, most creators figured out that social media was a multimedia pursuit. Twitter was where the writers were, and Tumblr was for the heady, long-winded explorations of self and interest. Viners had six seconds to capture your interest and the quickest way to do that was playing to the base—your lowest common denominator. King Bach's main focus was race, making himself the butt of watermelon jokes: that kind of thing. He wasn't celebrated often, but he was insanely popular, growing almost twelve million followers. The popularity of his accounts got him access to celebrity and money: the kind of power that told other people the formula for success on Vine was this particular caricature that, for all purposes, seemed to be "selling out."

Kenny's first two years of the app, he wasn't popping. There wasn't an explosive start to his career as a content creator that others found. However, what he found was the respect of people whose power floated close to his own. That first year, Kenny received his first paid deal from a rapper. It was only twenty dollars, but he was in high school back in Detroit and that kind of money can get you something for lunch.

Kenny's ambition pushed him in a direction that many do not realize is a core part of the multimedia experience that is content creation. He joined groups. Some of the first people that Kenny connected with was King Vader (1.5 million followers), who would become a director after the shuttering of Vine, and Jay Versace (6 million followers), whose career as a DJ and producer would see a renaissance; Versace produced for Lil Yachty's *Lil Boat 3.5*, Tyler the Creator's *Call Me If You Get Lost*, Sza's *SOS*, and Doja Cat's *Scarlet*. He'd eventually become a Shorty and BET Award–nominating,

Grammy Award–winning artist. Though he is no longer a content creator, Jay Versace never dropped his name: his brand, his first identity as a creator.

At the time, these people were hoping for the clout that could build their names and futures and that would take work: constantly. Daily uploads that would keep their numbers growing.

"I was posting every day, gaining thousands of followers every day. I'd notice that if I didn't post, I'd only get about three hundred followers a day, so I had to make sure I didn't stop."[2]

I interviewed Kenny Knox in the same room with the faint blue walls and basketball paraphernalia that was in every one of his vines at the time. He learned the tools of his particular art form: a cellphone, lights, things like that. He had to lo-fi most of his tools since he was still in high school and he was still playing sports—soccer, mostly. He told his principal that he would have a million followers by the end of the year, and if he did, he would need to buy his classmates a pizza party.

The principal agreed.

Most of Kenny Knox's growth came from these Black creators who supported him in these small groups. Most weren't exactly friends; others would eventually become them. Kenny was connected to his longtime collaborators Demetrius Harmon and Dopeisland in those chats, who he didn't know also lived in Detroit and thus were perfect for collaborating in the same way most creators in New York or Los Angeles were.

Harmon and Dopeisland had their own brand. Their videos played off their relationship really well. Harmon was the softer personality; Dopeisland torpedoed forward. They seemed to have a healthy intimacy between them that validated deep wants of their Black audience. Eventually, Harmon would drop his You Matter line and move to Los Angeles, but that would not have been half as successful without the relationships he cultivated here in this moment.

Kenny's success flourished under the Black Viners of these groups. He had an example to follow. When Jay Versace put things on his head rather than buying a wig, others followed. When Demetrius Harmon started making consistent skit series, others followed. When Kenny started his brand of humor, jokes within the jokes of Vine, others found ways to emulate it. Better, now they had an older community who could set the standard of what to expect once they all graduated.

He worked with type of open and accelerated people who would put together something like the Florida Super Vine—a beach retreat for twenty-somethings that imitated Freaknik of the '90s. The debauchery discussed of that weekend doesn't even exist in most of the remaining compilations. Not much content was generated in this event, but Kenny remembers watching what could be once he grew up with a significant enough platform on this app. This was Black Vine, a machine of near constant innovation in under six seconds. Creators had to be writers, directors, producers, and editors all rolled into one. Also, because a lot of creators were not receiving the brand deals upfront—they also had to market and negotiate their own deals if they ever got one.

Kenny eventually made it to his goal. He found his niche in nostalgic humor—the kind of thing that is catnip to millennials. At the time, the style of instant humor relied on making art about art. In 2015, a Little Einsteins' trap mix hit the internet. If TikTok had been a thing, it would've been considered a viral sound. The video dropped February 23rd, 2015, and was captioned: "When you go on the popular page and all you see is little Einsteins vines."

Kenny hit the height of his power afterward: without as many brand deals as his white counterparts or the general lack of interest. He engaged his audiences; he worked at it . . . and then something odd happened.

Kenny Knox made the top vine list with only eighty thousand views on a video: one of his goals at the time.

It was out of the ordinary: worth celebrating. However, most videos that popped up on this explore-page-like feature were somewhere in the millions or at least the several-hundred-thousand range. With such low views, it shouldn't have been possible.

It was the first trumpet of a platform dying.

Kenny went on to win the last Viner of the Year Award ever.

Vine announced that the app would be shuttered in 2017 when buyers in the signing room pulled out of the deal. Most of the Black creators on the app had abandoned the site months before. This was something like the writing on the wall. When Black creators flee, there is no soul to a space. These were the people who created the content that filled the site surrounding the larger posts. Yes, big creators make high-quality work or they receive the vanity that people chase, but that is the role of capitalism in most things: to take credit for what really happens among the people and to give others this idea that what they have is achievable with hard enough work. The upper-levels perks ran out when the people they stood so far above vanished and, without the capital of something like Vine, they became tractionless. King Bach struggled to maintain an acting career for a while, becoming something of a meme for Uncle Toms in this new era. No creator said out loud they wanted to be like him, because to do so in an age of digital wokeness was tantamount to admitting you were a sellout waiting to happen.

Kenny was one of the last people on the app, out of sheer perseverance. Once he left, Kenny started building his world out on Instagram. He had his followers meet him there and eventually Kenny reclaimed most of the follows he lost on that app. He started getting brand deals, he moved to Los Angeles, but there were distractions in these spaces—the kind of emptiness anyone who moves to Los Angeles finds.

See, moving to Los Angeles when you are a social media personality has hang-ups. The entertainment industry has its pathways set up so much and so beaten that anything divesting from the power it incorporates can be dangerous. The space between opportunities becomes larger. Other creators—who make videos of the perks and advantages—find themselves being diminished into salesman. If that isn't your goal, and if you, say, had cultivated a career of short-form humor like what was found on Vine, you will struggle for longer. There is a TikTok of a popular choreographer training younger dancers at his studio, where he reminds them all that competition dancing and touring requires something even the most skilled TikTok dancers lack: stamina. You need to dance for almost two hours straight: you need lungs and muscles that will not give up on you in the middle of that. And, yes, these dancers are fantastic at creative and expressive moves that most traditional dancers cannot emulate: they will not likely lose work knowing that no show will be for under two hours.

The TikTok dance pipeline cannot sustain these people at best. And, at worst, there isn't room for a dancer who steals attention.

When I moved to Los Angeles, the first thing I made sure to do was try to figure out where the Black people lived and how. They were down in Inglewood, mostly, doing their own things to get back. I went to the Jean-Michel Basquiat exhibit and saw how that man was living when he was in his prime: painting and pondering. I entered the musty recreation of his painting studio with a luxury trench coat thrown over splattered paint as if he could replace it easily. I saw maps of where he would eat in New York and LA; I saw the dance halls he loved to DJ in; I saw no mention of his queerness. I knew it was packaged better that way. I realized how much packaging was going on around me once I stepped outside because talent was not enough—I'd need a blue check, too, and a lot of humility and willingness to accept things won't look like the promised land I dreamed of online. This was the real entertainment industry: built behind walls I had to shatter to even see.

Kenny Knox navigated similar stations trying to act or perfect his comedy skills. His old friends either doubled down or phased out: Harmon left content creation in favor of the odd TikTok video or Live to promote his mental health fashion company; Jay Versace became a musician. Knox himself stayed in Los Angeles for as long as possible while phasing in and out of creative funks. Eventually, Knox moved back to Detroit to figure out what he could be doing to better align his purpose and his art for a space where social media felt unsure. He started trying to find a way to make the hard work a little less hard, and a little more like the reason he joined something as simple as Vine in the first place.

//////////

Black people aspire to the mainstream for protection.

It's not that we are all in danger. There are a number of blocks I can walk down where I am safe if all the faces are brown, like mine. It's a sanctity of spice and cologne, loud laughter of cracking thunder, power in the skin, leaping from touch to touch like copper wire under lightning.

We proclaim these meccas our streets. The red carpet is rolled out, and we trod barefoot across the sleek velvet. We share one song, if not one voice, and we dance across concrete in celebration of things that have already happened or might come. As I remember one bitter course, Ethnic American Literature, where a tall fifty-five-year-old white man inquired about Black concerns, asking me: "Do you ever hate being Black? With all that you faced?"

I smiled, in that way where lemon juice was fresh in a new Black wound. And I responded that, at least for me, I do not find myself interrupted in my love of my Blackness. I find myself interrupted when there are people who find repulsion to that. I cannot hate myself because of the ways other people are disgusted: I frankly do not think about white people that much to do that.

Two years later, I learned about Toni Morrison's work and her beautiful premonition of Ohio, as a place where Black folk find joy and communities are erected with their own traumas that fall on grown-wounded child hearts. It's Black as hell. But I also see their eyes linger, sticking like salt to ice cubes on house and home.

I see a Black girl treading through a small kingdom with glistening floors and polished treasures—a hall of white wonders. If the white gaze is the unquestionable conquering of perspective, rooting itself behind every lens, a Black gaze is the yearning for safety. In a home with seats of leather and cloth as warm as chocolate and as smooth as a mayfly's wings.

The Black gaze is what young rappers see through when they lie in bed and dream of an escape. The Black gaze is at the center of every Oscar ceremony, at the end of Grammy season. It's Black excellence. It's Black exceptionalism.

Artists in the digital age are beholden to this same idol worship and dream.

6

Each one, teach one.

—A BLACK EDUCATOR

IT'S BEEN DONE BEFORE

In 2020, we crowned Generation Z the TikTok generation because it was funny to see that they really thought they created something new. A part of the blame belongs to millennials, who failed to pass on the pertinent information of our legacy. Sadly, we've learned from our own elders that at times it's easier to keep kids entertained than it is to keep them engaged. However, the problem with failing to teach is that things slip through a lot of cracks, and for Black folk, the things often found in those nooks and crannies are gems—lessons we cannot afford to forget.

We should've explained that Vine came first and Vine maintained a culture of Black folk being robbed of their due.

At one point, Forever 21—a popular retailer at the time—was flush with shirts, hoodies, and jerseys with a million quirky one-liners each based on easily meme-able moments. What's not found on the receipts or clothing tags along the neckline are the names of the Black folks who went into these moments.

The idea that the internet could be a commodity did not exist when the conversation was purely about Black kids. As was the case during the eras of early American music, when Black artists composed a large majority of the sounds that became pivotal to establishing white America in the US and abroad. Rock 'n' roll being the most optimum of sounds that became dynamic once white musicians learned to string a guitar and stud a jacket, but it's happened to every single genre and it likely won't stop happening until there aren't any more Black people to steal from.

Last week, I saw a white man lace up a durag on Instagram. A week before that, a white woman started a soul train line. The use of trap drums has become a staple in white pop music, and the latest American music sweetheart has a verse from Quavo or someone exactly like him on her first album. The appeal of Black credibility is trafficked when Black people are stolen from. The appeal of Black credibility has more traction in any genre of art in the twenty-first century than any one singular gimmick.

Even literature isn't too distanced from similar escapades, as Black authors are denied daily advances and opportunities offered to white authors who merely appropriate the Black perspective (researched) that Black authors have been writing on their entire careers. The irony within this appeal toward Black credibility is solely reliant on the truth that Black identity is found best when watered down through virtually any other culture.

I'm reminded of Zora Neale Hurston at times of critical intrigue, like meditating upon the nature of Black Art theft. I sit with her spirit, picturing little white cat burglars running through a temple of black mosaics, smearing greasy fingers on priceless treasures they'll sell for pennies on a market that just won't get it.

The Black children of technology are no more strangers to this phantom of "mediocrity" than they are to the perils of the internet. It's their womb. It's a hidden state of their development tucked so cleanly between the latency and genital. For Black youth, it becomes a second language. A beautiful concept because of the ways Black

Americans were denied a tongue of our own, created in our seclusion, in our safety—at home.

Over the summer of 2019, I mentored a group of twenty-two kids from across the United States. There were a handful of Latine kids—a Cuban American girl with a radiance and a Mexican boy fresh from Texas—and a single white one. The rest of the class was Black, and passionate and proud of their Blackness. They laughed when their spirits were high, like rolling thunder and fire burst. They jeered when their spirits low—they lashed out with lightning, and they deserved love in all of its small places.

In the months preceding our meeting at the University of Miami, I had swarms in my stomach. It is well documented that I'm fascinated with mentorship. Black children of any age deserve the rights and access to the experiences that so many others absorb by the sole power of proximity. My personal mentees, Brandon and Justin, say I do it well—but I believe it's simply the natural glamour of proximity. We were only three years about in age when they met me; they understood the circumstances that could create someone like me—bisexual, Black, and, allegedly, brilliant. They also didn't need me.

Teenagers of the time were different. I had no real idea what the hell I was doing there. The program specialized in residential real estate. I was a writer whose claim to fame was articles in *Essence* and on MTV News. Five of the students had started their own businesses as résumé builders. I only got my first job as a punishment for shattering the gymnasium glass door in high school.

On our first day, a fight broke out between two childhood friends over a sports injury. I believe girls were probably involved, since they were both from Philadelphia and my own quirky past in the City of Brotherly Love said that when it came to women and the process of obtaining women, brotherly love didn't often exist.

That first day ended with a hospital visit to stitch the student incurred from the brief match. A quick walk around the scene revealed blood smeared across the wall's surface. The governing powers of the university expected the eviction of the boys as soon as humanly possible.

They composed their own language for the boys.

FINDING COMMUNITY

At home, my front door was not as open to strangers as it was to kin. We kept those we didn't know on the opposite end. The threshold didn't greet anyone who did not know our knock and if we did greet you, it was with a timer set to when you'd be gracing an exit.

Community was always someone you suspected. And, so, it was community I learned to long for most.

Joining social media as a Black creator was something of a coming-out then, because in this world of light and mirrors there is an eye-opening naissance to the first moments of joining this world as one called to make, rather than one called to consume. It isn't something that you just start doing. I know plenty of visual creators whose teeth were cut in doing free fan works online for mutuals and the great talent who inspire their fandom. I hear stories of the graffiti artists in New York from my uncle Bobby, who thinks back to how utterly talentless he was but how equally desperate he was to impress the friends. Stories of my mother whose confidence, danger, and bravado lined up all sorts of opportunities across the streets. Uncle Bobby had some talent in illustration, whereas my mother and grandmother conjured skill from their tongue and persuasion. He painted the walls of his Oslo-blue bedroom with strong onyx letters from window to window and wall to wall. He taught us the song he'd sung while painting it, a song he'd sung since he was a child.

"Nobody loves me. Nobody likes me. I think I'll eat a worm."

It was a little schoolyard chant about loneliness and feeling unwanted. Unloved. Unacknowledged. Maybe even unattended. Sometimes, he sings these songs while driving as a trucker. I wonder if these are the songs he sings when he crashes the truck again on the road and strands himself in the cold wild of the Midwest.

He taught us more songs. These are less schoolyard, and because of that the lyrics stick less gracefully. They were his rap tags, his go-to verses in case he was ever asked to freestyle, and he had to lie like he was down when he was never going to be. My uncle Bobby had many jokes like a checkered harlequin and even more escape tricks like a magician. I suppose the only difference between a magician and a harlequin is whom their tricks serve.

He could do little close-up tricks with paper, folding and tearing them into all sorts of bizarreness. My uncle Bobby talked about graffiti taggers like my American Literature professor talked about the Founding Fathers—with the awestruck glamour of a fan. He talked about gangs of taggers he rolled with in Philly who introduced him to loose strippers and looser women. He recalled, in great detail, how paint and ink burst against cement blocks, sharp contrasts of red and green, blurring into the overlap as purple kissed bruises. He spit on the beatfreaks in Kangol hats and bomber jackets. Some in leather fedoras with shiny gold ice and chains. In the era of king crack and queen coke, he talked about the aluminum mist in someone's basement and the men who could get into upcoming rappers' studios and bankrolled mixtapes as shoddy producers for tracks that didn't top six blocks let alone radios. He talked about the ozone reeking from a fresh cone-spread of canned paint. He didn't know how to prime portrait boards or that a single coat was not enough to stick to the wall when it came time to paint over his masterpiece. We learned that our uncle liked to lie as often as possible for the entertainment of even a few in the room. But he always had a nugget of truth somewhere. I chose to see his truth in the art and in what it took to be a tagger. He grew up in Philly, where street art is in the iron of the city's brotherly love. Black Philly doesn't greet people with signs or the ringing of the bell, but brown-toned street art of mothers in ecstasy and Black babies with rotund, wet cheeks peering into the future. Of one planet on a perfect axis.

And Uncle Bobby said taggers were never supposed to be respected by anyone other than other taggers. That graffiti art is a wild style that is solely inspired by what's going down locally. Art can be global. Art should be global. But cannot forget the hand that deals its strokes. The hand might be motivated by the coin of kings, but how much of the work is meant to inspire the people? I cannot say how many private collections have been traded by the people whom we are told the art is for and worthy of, and who will never achieve the bliss of knowing their actual mistakes. I can say how every New Year, we share the graphic watercolor of a light-skinned woman in a fuchsia maxi dress climbing a stone stairway into the future, leaving behind her burdens and worries—knowing that when you are Black some troubles will always follow you. I can say this image is native to our people and its eternity. Something more than a meme, something that is aspirational.

But how many bills can aspiration pay? The water can't be heated with vibes and sensations. I'd also like to imagine one of my art friends told me art supplies ain't cheap. Pens cost a guap and so does Adobe Suites. The writers can debate the value of this content management system or that, but we will most often default to whatever is gonna be the most free.

As confident as my uncle was about his legend as a thief and a gangster, I know he has never put a penny down on paints and art supplies. Which tells me that they were either borrowed or loaned and forgotten in the long history of exchanges. Likewise, as the taggers in the late '80s found themselves at the bad end of legislative copycats of Mayor Abraham Beame's administration in New York. Their art was criminalized and, eventually, the call to create was silenced against the war on drugs and the harsh criminalization of Black men everywhere.

My uncle never pretended to have come close to seeing the inside of a prison. Not over that. But, as a dedicated poser, he lost something pivotal for his identity—the people he'd rather be spending his day with. The sight of hands against cold brick, focused behind bandanna masks as they filled the air with oily aerosol.

"There's family and then there's your friends. There's people who know you, but then there's also people who get you. That was what those early days were like. That was what hip-hop thought it could be."

Community does not just mean taggers and beatfreaks on the streets anymore. It's a premise that shocks older Black millennials and anyone else who survived the afterschool specials on cyberpredators and stranger danger. I watched *Degrassi: The Next Generation* at the time most of my peers were on MySpace, organizing their Top Friends list in accordance with whatever playground pettiness was going down: who was sitting with who on the school bus, who had whose neon sillybands on their wrist, who held hands with who at the roller rink. The first episode, Emma met a grown man at a hotel after he impersonated a boy her age who emulated her interests after snooping on her blog. By the end of the two-part episode, Emma learned to beware of predators online and to never divulge too much of her information online, not even in chat rooms. The producers returned to this message a few more times over the course of ten seasons. I imagine many older millennials learned some lessons about the distance to maintain with people online: that you should never mix too much pleasure in with even your business on there. This was an era before MySpace turned out the first content creators and influencers like Sean Kingston and Teyana Taylor, Soulja Boy became an overnight sensation with the Crank Dat movement, and YouTube accidentally made the earliest viral personalities. The concept of making money online was such a joke that *South Park* suggested that every viral sensation in the world is working for hypothetical money.

This is not the type of environment that promotes community with anyone you cannot touch, because like any mother has said—you never know. When the time comes to come together on all sorts of apps, no one comes thinking that they will meet new friends. Certainly, it isn't those who had to weigh their options on what they might lose by joining any public platforms. The earliest posts I come across are almost always reactionary. They remember old traumas Black folk faced. They prepare for new trauma we'll never see coming on or offline.

When the older members of Black Twitter were asked what the age of Twitter was like, they talk about how disjointed it was. Not a lot of people were followed or following outside of the sprees with strangers. The closeness was relative to some superficial quality. These people were in college, but they were also far out of collect, blossoming their careers as freelance journalists, stylists, and radio hosts. Not even podcasts were popular enough to truly be called a media form, and blogs were slowly fading out of the popular gaze.

Black Tumblr was different. Black Tumblr was almost exclusively about community. In fact, the very first thing you did was find community. Likewise, most of the demographic was my age. I joined Tumblr when I was fifteen. It piqued my interest when I realized the entire premise was near constant stimulation. Galleries of aesthetic mood boards and entirely too niche jokes. I got to diagnose myself as depressed and anxious when the suicidal ideation and the feelings of an overwhelming sense of death went unnoticed in a Black household. This was just before the strides to mental health awareness. I found master posts full of tips for new or amateur writers and other websites for pirating textbooks. It was a place of full details and context-ripened takes. It makes sense it was the place where I could find people. If anyone had their art "pop off" on there, I've never seen it. Luka Sabbat maybe. Luka was a fashion kid, with a style so eclectic it might as well have been designed for a mood board. He became the key item in so many pitch decks by brands trying to tap in with the millennials running the internet. His style was fit for his elf-like urban twink aesthetic: one moment, he was bohemian skateboard hip-punk, like a nymphic disk jockey at a '90s skate park, and the next draped in something knitted with an oval for a neck so it hung off the cliff of his shoulder as if caught in an intimate moment on a Sunday afternoon. He turned highly frill skirts into kilts, and blouses into weighty button-ups. Luka was a pioneer of this gender-fluid fashion era. Being the fashion-forward son of two well-connected style and taste curators, the fashion designer Clark Sabbat and former-stylist-now-chef Jessica Romer, he could accomplish a lot with a cigarette in his fingers and dreadlocks down his back.

This isn't to say his success was purely the fruits of nepotism or proximity. It is to say that where you come from, your community, can speak to your success in dozens of ways. Raw and unique talent is sometimes attributed to a community that made the best of what they had. Sometimes refined and traditional moods and poses are the fruit of an upbringing in which such an aesthetic is the church you gave your grace to as a child. Though the one credited with "discovery" here is Kevin Amato.

With an aesthetic born and bred in New York, Kevin tries to reprioritize beauty in men, particularly Black and Brown men found around New York. And, despite the Blackness implicit within Amato's artistic gaze, Sabbat had a career that seemed, like his crew, to take Blackness into the digital space but left the politics by the wayside, despite how implicitly the Black aesthetic revolves around the fight for liberation in the space where it reigns. You'd think, for Luka, that would be the digital one. To the contrary, in 2018, Luka himself twote:

> Back in 60's and 70's being a activist and being politically correct WAS the counter culture
>
> It has turned into the norm

Back then, people actually had to be in the streets and live this shit

It was a punk lifestyle in a way

There was actual consequences for being that back then . . .

So now that being an activist seems easier even though there are still real activists that really live this shit everyday.

There's big steps in being a real activists, it's a lifestyle and a huge undertaking.

But doing it on the Internet is the easy way out.[1]

Luka, being ephemerally moody and flighty with his thinking, might have changed his mind since posting this. But in all of these years he seldom tweets and has left it up. Perhaps this is him cementing his sense of community: not as one where accountability and protest are rewarded, but one where a man is nostalgic for the past, where everything is better and unobtainable. Perhaps he is nostalgic for what it meant to be an activist back when it was dangerous. Totally unlike activism today, when being an activist even on the internet has claimed not just lives but futures and families.

Still, most regard Luka Sabbat as Victor Abloh's chosen heir, the kind of kid who could take not only Black fashion but fashion in its wholeness by its horns. He hung out with some unsavory people, though, like Ian Connors, who'd become the center of a lot of sexual assault accusations years before the #MeToo movement claimed Bill Cosby and Harvey Weinstein, and before *Surviving R. Kelly* pulled the Pied Piper of R&B off his perch and into the mud. He wasn't too impacted. Luka Sabbat would appear on *Grown-ish* as a key love interest for Yara Shahidi's Zoey Johnson character. It was exciting, but Luka Sabbat was too cool. He thought social media activism was just slacktivism and that slacktivism changes nothing. I wrote a missive on him. And from that take and the uncomfortable sort of person he spent his time with, Luka Sabbat softly and slowly faded into the background of the fashion industry until he popped up again in 2023, aged and chunkier. The magic softly vanished like the dimming of cigarette flame on the butt of the rolled shaft.

//////////

Two of my longest mutuals on social media found me in a hashtag for *Vampire Diaries* on Tumblr. One, living in Jamaica, whom I would share *Charmed* and *Buffy* hot takes and GIFs with, slowly vanished from my line of sight as the app slowly died after the ban on sex content. The other followed me across several new apps and entered a near intense flirtationship after a while. We never actually crossed any social lines or met in person. I know when I see his post-gym selfies with his solid brown eyes on the camera and the body I've seen him sculpt from start to prime, I send him heart eyes and a smile. He sends me a hearts emoji. We laugh together until he asks me 'bout my book.

I know of many others on Tumblr who've followed me to others after Tumblr fell. They understood the rules and way of life that'd come with having to merge these two spaces. One, who was a gym-loving anime nerd with no other discerning personality traits started posting fitness nutrition menus in-between advocating for his country music albums. He found more traction when he tweeted out against colorism and on the anniversary of Trayvon Martin's death. I found out he dated another of my friends, a content creator who would eventually pivot into the online pleasure industry. And by "dated," I mean in the loosest terms of the word, because they are queer biracial Black men and they have a lot of discussions on what qualifies a relationship when you are treated as a sexual deviant while being seen as a racial deviant. You can share your body with a friend. You can also share your body with a friend who you don't know you're dating, or a date you don't know is just a friend. It's confusing. In the end, they together learn how aware this little mutual is and knows how they might try to perform activism because of what that little mutual experienced on

Tumblr—a place where if you were self-righteous enough you could milk communities for the type of social capital that could turn into money and noteworth. The industry can be that fickle, sadly. People just want to seem like they care, and if they are seen among the right people, who are talking about the right things, they can get that.

I think about his romanticization of this era when I remember that first call for writers to join Snacktivist's group chat on Twitter. Snacktivist was a Black writer. Perhaps more prominent than my peers in the digital writers' era. At the time, we hadn't even decided if we'd be properly referred to as "culture writers" or "digital writers," but we recognized the job description as being at the middle of the road between reporter and blogger. A good clean start for a writer hungry enough in ambition and guts. To observe the flow of experiences across the timeline and have enough skill to speak on it.

Snacktivist was Black and a New Yorker. But he also had the dangerous quality that makes one particularly suited to social media: loneliness. That overwhelming cold specter that rests where you sit and denounces every exploit as a shallow plea for victory, which is another name for deep-seated yearning and the dedication to see it through. Snacktivist had tweeted his way into a level of supremacy ahead of the rest. He also followed paths into outrage and conflict. People debated him and fought him and came up with power, like many Black people have online, but he had a community for it and when community is present in an action, it becomes an art.

In this community, outrage had a tactic. An explosion in one space, shared to others, becomes a nuclear detonation. Perhaps there's a battle cry like "Groupon peen" or "Talcum X" before the boom. Perhaps it is eloquent, language scribbled across 130 characters into a cheap sucker punch as a punctuation. By the end of the whole ordeal, someone has gone silent—it is a kind of public execution, which bleeds across the timeline and a corpse that will rise again, eventually, bruised. I have never looked at the subject of these collective lashings the same way after. I don't think we're supposed to. But those who did the lashings came out stronger, as if feeding on the spree blood ruptured from these souls.

This spectacle was not always bloody. Freelance Digital Journalists often had an issue tracking account payables for our finances and when Net40 became something closer to a Net60, twelve voices calling on a publication could convince most corporations to do much better controlling their timetables. These writers do not care much for capitalism. They compare it not to a tail-biting hydra but to the poison that kills the hydra, its tail, its prey, and the fungus that will strip the flesh from bones and soften the calcium into a grassy knoll. Nothing survives. Nothing benefits. Nothing grows. But it is the reality we must face, so we must drink our poisons and build our tolerance likewise.

I used to tutor him on his writing and the finer details of the craft over long four-hour chats. It was my craft, too, so I knew a lot about character and suspense and how writing must always please the author first and the reader inevitably: that grammar has nothing to do with storytelling but everything to do with the storyteller. He used to criticize how my drafts did not use double-line spacing as an issue of accessibility for those reading it, rather than a practice decision for me to measure metrics. We had a disagreement in our time after Demetrius Harmon went viral for his first negative reason over me and the issues of plagiarism. Our relationship was never repaired once I refused the process of blood.

This is not a tidbit about the carceral nature of callout culture or a case for cancel culture where people fail to hold up to their own morals in service to their reputation. This is instead about my first important lesson on community online that I learned after years hunting for it.

It cannot exist. Not eternally. Because where platform is born, people become placeholders. We do not know the better of one another until we have seen one another dressed in the fires of our own contempt. We cannot know each other as people until we know how one another bleeds.

WHO'S THE AUDIENCE FOR THIS, ANYWAY?

I once heard Toni Morrison preach about the white gaze. I say "preach" not to disrespect one of the most powerful Black women in history. I say "preach" because when she spoke in front of the dented blue of her background, I surrendered. Her voice carried the quaking of a stern, unbending forest. The kind that is cold and dark in the pitch-black evening. The kind that shot straight up to the stars like flag-poles and whose leaf blades felt as freezing as steel during the harsh work of winter.

God is where the mind seeks the spirit, holding hands to form a person whose entire being is struck by lightning. Toni Morrison was a preacher, and some did not know this about her. In her time, Black art was moving toward empowerment. Black was beautiful. Black was excellent. Black had a stern spine and an uncompromising disposition. Toni Morrison was not universally loved, lauded, or praised. In fact, Toni Morrison is one of the first Black authors I ever committed to memory, and it was because of the grotesque book bans she faced early in her life. It was the first inkling of a trend regarding Black authors marching toward any modicum of success. It is a way to dictate whose truth can be received. I learned who Toni Morrison was because of a list of books that I couldn't read. I was not yet the rebel I felt in my spirit; I did not read those books. I would eventually in college: these books became the canon for Black literature for all my would-be students. It became my bible while truth was my religion. I was shocked when I learned others did not find even one of Morrison's truths on their hands. These folk who could not find someplace to be in the small worlds rendered larger by her words, and how they danced free of her.

When *The Bluest Eye* hit shelves, it was unflinching. Black men took some exception at the time to what Black women had to say. My grandmother, a devout lover of the Black man, criticized *for colored girls who have considered suicide / when the rainbow is enuf* by Ntozake Shange. She said that it did not paint the Black man in the best kind of light. We watched the film adaptation and the atrocity cut so intermittently that they might as well be staccato on a music sheet. Back-to-back men with the blade, women licking bleeding flesh. Rape-slash. Lie-slash. Abandonment-slash, physical-slash-violence-slash, stabs of betrayal, lacerations of biological dishonesty and the twisted handle of emotional oblivion. They are recognizable without having to say it out loud—as the plights of the Black woman twenty-years before the wider use of a word like misogynoir.

She asked who was the audience for such a story, as the men around her had done so similarly.

Six years prior, Toni Morrison had published *The Bluest Eye* and many men asked much the same questions. Some have suggested Toni Morrison was inspired by her experiences at Howard University: the flagrant self-hatred, colorism, and misogyny of the Black men of a certain age who would be powerful save for one crucial detail of their birth. But Toni Morrison has spoken so fondly of this time and the men she was surrounded by that this could not be a whole truth even if we traffic in a culture where all we need are substantial ones.

I once read records that were scanned and rescanned black and white of the August 15, 1970, *Kirkus Reviews* that called *The Bluest Eye* a good read. In a following characterization of Pecola as a "sparrow," her fall is blamed on the lack of a proper overseer. Immediately, it is clear that the audience for this book is misaligned. Scholar Leroy Staggers analyzes a list of review publications that include *Publisher's Weekly*, the *New York Times*, the *Times of London*, the *National Observer*, *Newsweek*, the *New Yorker*, *Booklist*, *Choice*. Staggers highlights how misaligned the audiences really are too: he looks at the lavish praises put upon Morrison but cannot fathom where the understanding aligns. It is as if he asks how? How can these white people understand Pecola? How can they understand the danger? How can they feel the words of this story—how it invalidates their existence—blossom the dedication that they have to turn the tale out onto the world? Concrete roses have had a better chance becoming a bush than it is for these words of oppression to be fully digested by those inflicting the wound of it. Not immediately, anyway. It takes practice, the gradual cracking of the stone, the undermining of bias and point of view. The realization that something, finally, is not about you.

Years later, Percival Everett would publish *Erasure*; in turn, the film *American Fiction* would be adapted. It asks questions of white audiences and fans of Black work: it asks why exactly do they care so much for Black atrocity upon Black bodies? Why do they care for Black depictions from the gutter? Why do they care for race if it's only how lucky they are to opt out of it?

Leroy Staggers highlights that it was the publication *Essence* that first recommended this book for Black readers, sympathetic to the direct and subtle ways racism is to blame for the protagonist's fate. Because there is overt racism, the chemistry of niggers and legislation and there is subvert racism, the chemistry of gender, sexuality, and Blackness: together. That this is not merely the work of critics interested in Black art, but audience in conversation.

Black folk ask a question from time to time: Who is this for?

It's one of those haints I've become familiar with. I call them "haints" for some odd fascination with ghosts and spirits, but also because they spook the timeline so often. They leap out at you when your finger catches the grid and slides like ice just a few notches south. Topics jump right at you.

I can't tell you the first time I came across it. It's as ancient as dating rules, dinner with Jay-Z or $10K, and other rules of disengagement made up by digital outlanders who live in Atlanta, tweeting between the times of 1 p.m. and 3 p.m. They've asked the question about many things, but mostly things they've never seen.

The original airing of the HBO Max series *Lovecraft Country* was my favorite, because it was a period where the past was made innocent by art's increasingly digital foothold. See, we, the timeline, would consume art as a family, which means live or streaming, we would watch motion pictures together on the timeline. I would learn the word "kairos" in undergrad to describe the way timing operates within arguments, and kairos was everything to watching something as family. It is because you will get reactions you only can interact with in a timed, parasocial manner. And the conversations could be dry or fresh. It could make a show or break it. It could change the trajectory of the entertainment industry. But, mostly, it was pleasurable to not feel alone in your interests: that other people agreed that what you liked was something worth being passionate about.

HBO's *Lovecraft Country* are to this day the only people to send me an influencer kit. They were the first people to remember that authors on Twitter have influence, and it paid off. This kit was a fancy box designed like a crate, filled to the brim with paper straw. Every time I reached into the box, I found a new treasure: a copy of *Lovecraft Country* by Matt Ruff, a South Side Science Futurists Club sweatshirt, a pair of circular rim Bohten sunglasses, a Bright Black Sundown candle, Ta-Nehisi Coates's novel *The Water Dancer*, Tomi Adeyemi's *Children of Blood and Bone*, and a Life on Autopilot custom bag. We also received an e-screening for an early stream of the first episode of *Lovecraft Country*. I wrote a review for *Cassius Life* as my great tribute and waited for it to be late to premiere. I love it: *Lovecraft Country* was everything I wanted in speculative media. Not the transphobic storyline concerning a two-spirited character, or the questionable approaches to consent, or the shameful colorist and triggering ways of the production, but the drama of a world filled with magic navigated by Black folk who are increasingly disillusioned by how whiteness employs it. How it was a series that catered only to the die-hard Black fans of pulp fiction who were forced to contend with the racism of the everyday creators of such marvels—no longer trying to *ignore* the problems while also not apologizing for loving something in spite of them.

Not everyone saw the grace in this. Every week we logged on to the timeline to watch this show as a family and endured as many people as possible forget that this is a *drama*. A story told as sadly as possible. It was not always dedicated to painting its protagonists as heroes, but as human beings struggling every moment they take up space.

Atticus Freeman, the protagonist of the series played by Jonathan Majors, is positioned as a "good man" throughout the series' first few episodes. Despite Atticus's smarmy jealousy, sexual insecurities, homophobia, and ambivalence to the casual violence around himself, he is a "good man." At the time, Jonathan Majors was relatively unknown outside of a few great films. It was really easy to take him for face value when he wakes as a US soldier on a segregated bus ride back home to Chicago and carries the belongings of a Black woman that he was just speaking to into the city when that bus breaks down and a white pickup comes to ferry the white passengers the rest of the way. This is the Midwest, not the South, but there are certain expectations all the same about how you get down when Jim Crow sets the tune.

The audience had been in love with him. Perhaps too much. They wanted him to be some kind of superhero and for this to be a cookie-cutter adventure where we win in the end and our extra-magical powers bring a smile upon our faces. They waited for this moment to come. I knew it wouldn't. I might not have read the source material in its entirety until I received the book in that influencer kit, but I knew that is not how H. P. Lovecraft's stories go.

It isn't until we see Atticus do something we already knew he did as a character that the timeline turned on him and thus the show. We watched him stroll up to a tortured Korean nurse and put a bullet in her head in his fight against communist South Korea. We watched him join his brothers in arms as the US replaced other factions as an occupying demon in the east.

As an instrument of the US Army, Atticus slaughtered communists in South Korea with cold expressionless tactics. We watched his ruthlessness as he justified his actions as for the well-being of Korea. Or how he highlighted the segregation Black soldiers face within the US military.

Throughout the episode, you come to realize that Misha Green, the show's creator, is processing something. An empathy that is so profound I would not know it until I see Amy Tan, the prolific author of *The Joy Luck Club*, recounting the love she had for her mother despite the abuses and circumstances of her childhood. It is with tenderness that she remembers her grandmother's life as a concubine, suffering and silent, or her mother enduring her first husband's atrocities, suffering and silent. Throughout the series, she has always considered Atticus with a patience that flowers in seasons. Every episode, we feel that tempo and hold out hope because Misha, our writer, holds out hope. She isn't a stranger to writing troubled characters, after all. She has written for *Sons of Anarchy*, *Heroes*, and *Spartacus*. These are stories of antiheroes, but a certain kind of antihero—Atticus is a new one. One who loves openly with his arms out wide and who smiles and cries. He is a good man, but. It is coming from a culture of buts, where Black women have made space for the exception because the world will not, and it is their duty as good women to do so.

It is a but that we viewers recognize.

The timeline declared that they were not the audience for this despite how many once sympathized with their grandfathers who fought in the Korean War. Despite how many Black men highlight Korean fried chicken being a relic of Black Americans entering the global chessboard through our participation in these historic atrocities.

And though the episode, "Meet Me in Daegu," is a story of two monsters rendered in this way by their neglectful parents falling in love and fumbling through the terms of their monstrosity, we are left with an audience who are unwilling to make that final step into speculative questions. What comes next after the monster takes off his mask and shows himself to be kin? Do we love him? Do we still hate our enemies?

The audiences had an answer, as unromantic as that is. It is far more romantic for a writer to have no answer. But that is not the digital age we live in. In this age, everyone has an answer. And it is always the right one. By the end of the season, an old mutual follower of mine who loved Black Art as much as I do—who stood for Black vampires when I stood for Black witches—unfollowed me because of a screaming match on the merit of this series with a random who disagreed with my appreciation of it: one that saw magic in the hand of Black people. The series never got a second season for a myriad of reasons: Jonathan Majors would be scrutinized in the media after a domestic abuse incident in NYC; other reports would state the use of Black face to darken light-skinned extras; critics would highlight the violence of killing off the show's only intersex, Native American character and the execution of casual homophobia. Several writers would say *Lovecraft Country* was canceled due to a toxic work environment, and, worse, Michael K. Williams would pass years later due to a drug overdose from a combination of fentanyl and heroin after a lifetime of addiction struggles. He would report difficulties following his work on *Lovecraft Country*.

Audiences are the ones who decide what is right. They consume with their attention, and the attention economy is a device of perpetual motion. There's a thirst for it in this new generation. In a world where adrenaline rushes to the tips of your fingers, just after an era where Blackness in distress became snuff films that end in a flash as fast as the police who cross the box onto the screen. We watched

George Floyd's murder on the TL (timeline) just three months prior to the debut of *Lovecraft Country* and in the midst of a global lock-down. In a world of masks, the one face we saw clearly had the shock-ing streaks of a Black man's panic. The stakes in a world like this is that everyone must be fed: no matter how gentling the demands are or violent those demands are.

In this digital world, after an event like #OscarsSoWhite where April Reign (192.1k Twitter followers), a Newark, New Jersey–born media strategist and champion for diversity and inclusion pushed for the Oscars to second-guess what exactly led the Academy of Motion Picture Arts and Sciences to nominate no actors of color for two years in a row, for the Eighty-Seventh and Eighty-Eighth Academy Awards, and to maintain a lack of diversity again for the Ninety-Second Academy Awards. In this digital world, Black viewers come to the conclusion that it is entirely because of what the academy's current membership prioritizes in the stories they watch. It is entirely the audience considered by the membership, and not entirely the mem-bership itself. In 2016, the truth was that non-Black audiences loved a particular narrative, and typically Black works could involuntarily become caught up in these expectations.

In 2018, the battle cry reached down the timeline against slave films and other pictures depicting Black plight. It might be because we as Black viewers can become exhausted with the burden of the many ways our bodies can be broken—many that could barely embody the reality of these tortures due to the ugly constraints of something like censorship. It was also because certain entertainment became syn-onymous with whiteness. As if to say only someone looking to make white people feel good could like a particular media that made Black people feel bad. This is not the total truth.

To be fair, slave films have a caustic habit of becoming the only truth of Blackness. That is to say, it is the role that Black people are preferred to be seen in. If it isn't this, then it is also how the white gaze looks to consume the play of suffering in a sadistic way, the kind of ways that cause videos of Black children being beaten by impatient parents and schoolyard fights to go viral. And there were the stereotypes of mammies, sapphires, and jezebels dominating the image of Black women in media. After years of enduring this on screen and during the awards season, it's permissible why Black outlanders on the internet would want the trend to stop.

However, Black creators are attached to the speculative. The suggestion of a world where things can be understood as adequately as Black people understand racism: innately and with disgusted disdain. Where topics we talk about in barbershops and salons and on the timeline can be digested through stories by a storytelling people. It is a biased truth that we are all storytellers inherently by purchase of what we do with our hands and at the knees of our elders; it also turns us into something of a selfish critic.

Critics, unlike popular misconception, serve a role between the art and the audience, but none more so than the critic who is themself an artist. Who can see the paintbrush strokes on a canvas and rather than seeing the potential of the completed piece finds the pressure of an industry hungry for profit when content hits the galleries. Where art dies and creator becomes capitalist. These critics frown, jot down a note and prepare to face a world that will hate them for the demand that things be nothing less than perfect.

In this era, media consumers are also creators. Anyone with a smartphone, an email address, and access to the reactive imagination can read like a writer and watch like a filmmaker. Black connoisseurs have always had this outsider approach to the industry. Ice Cube started producing his own films in 1995 and thus for as long as I've been alive. He started his production company, CubeVision, for independence: to tell the stories that he most preferred to tell, centering Black people, our culture and our qualms. It was him who started the *Friday* franchise during a renaissance of Black TV and film in the

'90s—where Black comedians of the Phat Tuesdays in LA and the Def Comedy Jams were taking the industry to new heights.

By the height of Ice Cube's independent film era, people no longer knew Ice Cube as a slightly antisemitic rapper-poet from NWA, with an unbridled rage and unwillingness for compromise. As the fictional character Riley Freeman from *The Boondocks* put it: he was the dude who made family movies. Likewise, most Black readers would grow on platforms like Amazon into writers themselves in the genre of urban fiction; they wrote stories of Black women in desperation, in love, in power, and in plight. Stories that dominated Amazon's African American literature categories in a way no traditionally published stories could stop. Sometimes without even editors to clear out typos and errors. They didn't have the license of the writers within the mainstream they competed with, but they had the authenticity, and they knew the audience, because they were the audience.

It is likely these reasons why we ask questions of audiences when we do not sense the author having us in mind explicitly. We say, "Had it been me—" because had it been us the story would be better; it'd be about what we have to say; it'd be about what impacts our dreams when we are wide awake. Because the issues of some college kid can't speak to the hood, but the hood can't speak to the suburbs, but the suburbs can't speak to the country, because the country can't speak to the inner city. It's a lot to keep in mind when you are merely trying to coax an already fickle muse to labor for you.

I have watched friends flinch at the idea that their favorite story-tellers cannot perceive them through the mists of their own wonder and spectacle. Audiences matter when consuming art, where they can auction their time across the timetables in front of them; but we can make things for our kind of people. Our kind of people trust our work to speak for itself, for our pain to be on the page. They trust in the dialogue between the storyteller and the village, that they might not know and like every word on every line, but the heart will. The heart of the story is what the lover takes with them to share with those most willing to listen. When the Black artists speak to our uniform traumas on the page or across the screen, we come to a premonition of all kinds of hurt we as humans cannot escape. Not the vanity of brokenness, but the truth of experience. No audience can be in a creator's mind when they are creating authentically, because the truth of the matter is I do not believe any creator is sure the world understands how and why we hurt.

There's only one true answer I've come to when I see this question. I'll probably have it for the next time I see it.

If you had to ask, it just isn't for you. But someone's waiting for it.

7

The internet don't wanna heal you.

—A BLACK EXPERIENCE

SOMEONE SAID

Commentary became the hobby of social media sometime in early 2014. It was almost the inciting incident of why one joins platforms like Twitter. You have to have a point of view, and you now have people who will care. I imagine it had to come after a period of civil unrest, where everyone had grief and wanted nothing more than a way to talk about it, to understand it. When Trayvon Martin was murdered by a virtue-chasing civilian and Tamir Rice was gunned down in a flash of a second, people chimed in about their own trauma from guns. Back in Philly, men and women talk about the young brown-eyed children dying on the front stoop: about how they watched parks become cold and empty over the millennia because parks became the most unsafe place for a child to be.

In college, we looked at eloquence and diction like an actor—how emphasis on some words and gestures with others could mold an audience to do if not exactly what you want, angle them in a direction if everyone is sane—*if everyone is sane*.

Commentary online is not sane. It applies to everyone and everything. Perhaps it has something to do with how the social media landscape isn't real. It isn't real in the way people understand real to be something you hold because it's soft or release because it burns. Social media is an astral plane, a liminal space between real and unreal where things are not quite substantial. They're more than the theoretical is the actual. It is a reality people could only idealize in fiction—in the worlds of indigenous worldbuilding like the Dreamtime or the First World. It is here where everything we do becomes art and subject to critique. An image of your relationship randomly posted in pride becomes commentary for colorism. A general statement on the world becomes a weaponized PR statement. There is no escape to the gaze upon your actions and life, and this is more so for the Black artists of this time, whose world is defined by the microscope that hangs just over our head. The internet has a long memory, and conversation ends not with a period, but an ellipsis. It will be continued, eventually. And who you were before does not apply, because there is, sadly, profit to be had upon your name.

We call this phenomenon "the Discourse."

Eventually, this fascination would find its talents. *The Read*, hosted by Kid Fury and Crissle West, reached its audience when people needed to figure out how rage could be used, and in what way podcasts could take up space for people who didn't want to speak, but to listen. Stacey Dash appeared on *Fox and Friends* to become the Black voice railing against the Black majority as a treacherous supervillain. Gabrielle Union was the one in an online interview who reminded the world that she is the cousin of Dame Dash, who, while now railing against the Black Left for white executives and middle America, was a video vixen for Kanye West—who'd eventually suffer his own fall from grace.

Candace Owens (about 6 million Instagram followers), a young Black girl from White Plains, New York, came into the digital hemisphere in an unexpected way. In 2015, she became the CEO of Degree180, which featured a blog that covered a large variety of topics, including outright war against the racism of the Republican Party's many parties.

Essentially, Candace found her start by participating in discourse: politically or otherwise. Likewise, she went for something that Black commentators of the Digital Black Arts movement on YouTube like D'Angelo Wallace (1.72 million subscribers) would later criticize himself for targeting: the middle ground. It is an elusive train of thought that to be a well-rounded person, you listen to the perspective of everyone. The middle ground says that even people you don't wholesale agree with have something to offer where the truth of perspective can be found at the core of whatever rambling they've introduced. At that moment, D'Angelo Wallace revolved this self-critique around a YouTuber he once followed called Blair White, a conservative transwoman whose perspective leaned so right-wing that she labeled the Black Lives Matter movement as "trash" in a video, aligning with typical gender discourse of transwomen—especially that trans people are not trans if they do not undergo or work toward affirmation surgeries. Wallace felt that he was doing his due diligence toward rationality by listening to her. In truth, most of what he'd done was center the illusion of equal and unbiased discourse.

This is the same rationale that Candace Owens maintained for Degree180, where the guest voices did not limit themselves exclusively to progressive or conservative. Rather, it encompassed what any trained rhetorician would pursue: unbiased observation—even when we realize that anything unbiased is not necessarily correct or responsible. It was a generous gesture, though. Candace Owens advocated for the point of view of a conservative right-wing, despite having been the victim of a racist hate crime as a seventeen-year-old girl, and did more for her rising ethos as a personality and thought leader. This is capital in the social landscape that is the digital world, because your authority is always weighed against the fallibility of your beliefs. A neutral soul is thought to be the most resolute of spirits until they eventually pick a side.

In 2016, she launched SocialAutopsy.com for doxxing bullies online. Doxxing, a term for revealing the private and personal information of users online, is something of a controversial practice. Many victims—such as Black and Brown people who have been victimized online—see it as a tool of justice, revealing people who create unsafe environments online by hiding behind the anonymity of the internet. The internet is not always your friend; it is most certainly not always your community. There are people who will wage wars with you simply because there is a high to the kind of commentary that deconstructs a person. It is the filth of humanity, the gruel of the violent. They say it is their right in a public forum to say and do as they please with no repercussions: to live immortal on the hills that Jesus himself died on. Black women fight these immortal monsters often. Sometimes, they take the shape of Black men. It makes sense that Candace Owens would be the woman to feel the resonance of this online harassment and do something about it—no matter how extreme. Candace Owens at the time probably had a radical notion for this act. In the two years since Mike Brown's murder in Ferguson, when Don Lemon and journalists swarmed upon the Missouri town like mosquitos over a small pond, when DeRay came in a cobalt-blue vest and Black women tweeted a flame into the darkness of the internet with the resurrection of #BlackLivesMatter, we were all victims of the commentary. Friends turned former friends and family revealed deep cultural bias. Candace Owens was likely no different.

But that makes some assumptions that the world is somehow kinder to people when they are unmasked, as if monsters are always in hiding and weakened by cold air and light of day. Black women know better.

Eventually, Candace Owens would shed the pretense of this illusion and become something a bit more comfortable to her ambition:

a right-wing conservative activist, writer, and speaker. Candace's greatest hits include claims that the one hundred years following the abolition of slavery is the greatest the Black community has been since. She blamed socialism. Nothing specific about socialist infrastructure—just the nature of socialist thought entirely. Never mind the numerous bombings and desperate pushes to suppress the African American community between 1865, Juneteenth, and the Black Arts movement of the 1960s–70s.

How Candace described it, she became a conservative overnight. She "realized" that liberals were extremely racist and trolls. She was joined by Milo Yiannopoulous, a white gay man, and Christian Walker, the biracial "male-attracted but not gay" son of former NFL running back Herschel Walker. By the end of 2019, Owens had taken the trending page by storm, likely in relationship with President Donald Trump and the rising thirst for Black conservatives.[1] She launched the Blexit foundation in reflection (or parody) of the Brexit movement.

Owens was antagonistic in a way that you could only call "familiar." We've seen girls like this offline, on playgrounds, in our youth, popping bubblegum to remind us of all the ways we don't know how things should be. She'll say things—whether true or not—to put herself in the advantage. She cannot lose. She won't lose. And being right is less important than being powerful. There are certain kinds of conversations that are safe around her, and more sensitive ones that are not. She's a scary sort of person that doesn't truly have friends but is always around, somewhere.

She's one of the good ones. Her terror is what she says, not what she does. In the halls she'll listen and agree, not the haunts where she was born.

She'll diminish slavery to a minute issue that progressives take advantage of in a race war we cannot see anywhere in the world. At least, not in the way she describes as a Black woman speaking to Black people. She says that there were many myths to its construction. She believes that there were many, many white people—Republicans— who fought bravely to end the institution altogether because that is the inherent goodness of Ameritocracy: the blind and instinctual gravitation to goodness caused by good Christian values.

Conservatives aren't listening to her, but they know her sound-bites and clips. She parades halls online and offline that appeal to a strong right but more central point of view. They will call her one of the good ones.

This is the culture of commentary that swept social media following the death of Mike Brown—where the galvanization of the internet was around not only what we were talking about, but how we do it. Every hashtag after Mike Brown has been filled with this sort of ephemeral conversation. It's partially political, in that it is considering the ways race and culture interact on not just the physical level but the spiritual. It's partially passionate, because it asks the question of how Black people existing still today weigh on these comments beyond the stats and facts we can find in an infographic.

It makes sense that Candace Owens and the likes of her would find footing in a culture like this. During the Obama administration, *Fox and Friends* figured out how important a Black conservative mouthpiece was to seeding the discontent of the white majority without the unfortunate consequences of seeming racist in a "post-racial society." They used that phrase a lot—"post-racial society"—as if it meant something. It is a foible of the commentary art form to say things that mean nothing initially but upon chanting them in unison slowly become a thing. It used to be a tool that belonged to political commentary media like *Fox and Friends*. I learned this while watching *The Daily Show* and *The Colbert Report* in middle school when I should've been doing something more productive, like being called a nigger online. *Clueless* costar Stacey Dash adopted this role before Owens took the spotlight, but with the end of the Obama era, she was let go. She made one big attempt to return to the Black limelight afterward, playing a tongue-in-cheek femme fatale at the BET Awards. Subsequent articles made every pun of the word "clueless" for her. Her last big headline was accusing Jessie Williams of a "plantation mentality" for his widely celebrated BET Awards speech. Subsequent years, she's tried and failed a Senate career on the grounds of freeing people from similar "plantation mentalities" in a campaign that lasted just under a month; she opened up about a Vicodin addiction on *Dr. Oz*, who would also subsequently campaign for political power; appeared in *Roe v. Wade*, a 2020 film dramatization of the real-life case, which was reviewed as a hammy anti-abortion propaganda piece; and, finally, appeared in a sequel of the hit BET show *College Hill: Celebrity Edition*, where she tried and failed to return to college to receive her degree. Her final episode was smeared by Dash's inability to handle the criticism of her college professor for her largely unsubstantiated point of view. Her last major impression on the world was Dash giving an opinion to the applause of no one.

Dash lost even more footing when Donald Trump lost his 2020 reelection bid. Without an online presence, her power waned to almost nothing. Candace Owens did not have that problem. She's not just a paid commentator. She's also a content creator.

Her brand of content has never wavered from its source: a rhetorically equipped "good one." When Candace Owens logs on, she logs on to discuss a topic: abortion, immigration, antisemitism, racism, slavery, reparations. The topics she chooses are designed to incite, and they never fail to do so.

In 2018, the Netflix series *Dear White People* would satirize Candace Owens with the character Rikki Carter. Rikki Carter has violent beliefs against Black people as a Black woman and she is paid well for it. She becomes a chilling warning on the nature of commentary, because it is not a gig that exists with such cultural risks without reward.

Rikki Carter does not believe anything she says out loud, though she thinks strategically about what she says. Rikki Carter collaborates with her "opposition." She talks with the radical Black progressives on their media tours, calling in and calling out white hosts who profit off of the demonization of Black life on television—whom our protagonists champion. She can see how well connected a podcast like the show within a show, *Dear White P ople*, is to profiting from Black pain, even if it says otherwise. She knows that nothing you have to say out loud is altruistic, and she argues herself ahead of that human flaw first.

It was a depiction that stung a bit as someone who was platformed for similar commentary as Black writers tend to be now. Clarkisha Kent, Feminista Jones, Imani Bashir—many writers whose voices were known far before our writing ever was. Voices who fought the good fight online and paid for it. Or, perhaps, because of the nature of Twitter, it's always been known: evident in black and white and cyan, written between hashtags and never in a margin. And the words might fade, because nothing on an app made for such instant gratification and trading hands as flippantly as coin and cash can be immortal, the impression is there. You trust the ones who said it. You don't worry about the strength of the word when the argument has been made. The problem is that sharpens is the "why" of it all: Why are people listening? Why do they care? Why do we keep saying things far after the issue has become another issue? Is it the activism we care about, or is it the need to comment altogether?

Candace Owens has always profited from every one of her engagements, socially and financially. What she talks about has nothing to do with creation, the passion of working the truth to see if there is something new by the end of the work, but everything to do with capital.

TRÉ MELVIN

Shane Dawson made YouTube his playground back when the internet thought it didn't care about being PC. It was cooler to not care.

This is how I know that he knew what he was doing. There was no ignorance about where the power lay, or what jokes prodded more like a spear rather than a skewering needle. It was a caustic space. Tré Melvin did something a bit radical by showing he cared a bit more.

Artists don't often talk about space, because it is too harrowing to put to life the thing everything we do is centered on. It isn't just the white canvas of painting; it's the ambience we keep when we show the things we do. The oldest clip I've committed to memory is Erykah Badu on a stage enshrouded in mist, smiling. She was performing "Tyrone" live. In my memory, she's writhing a little as if the rock of her hips can enchant a serpent rising from a wicker basket. She looks out among a sea of Black faces, an unblossomed turban as high as her mental, lips the color of vermillion clay. Like a pastor, she calls on her brothers and sisters.

In four sentences, Erykah Badu sages the scene, purifying what will be a church of sharing and connection. We know what to expect when we are in Badu's atmosphere: spirituality, the kind of early aughts wokeness that people dream of in long locs and cotton, loose garb. The shea butter–type of lovers, but they live and survive on rent that barely seems fair let alone affordable just under streetlamps and between the scraping crash of city-metal and stone. We respect what we make as people is what we most wanted to attract. We arrive in Badu's space understanding that to bear witness is a gift, a present, because we are her kind of people. And she is ours.

Early YouTube had similar character with their space. It was a web of involvement in those days. There was no other app that really carried you on over to what you wanted to see externally outside of the everyday YouTube and MySpace.

How we used social media was less invested in social activism, less invested in getting involved. It was satire and comedy. The perfect place for early actors and comedians, a dangerous place for Blackness and self-assured existence.

Tré Melvin was not yet out of college.

Before he became Tré to a wider world, he was Edward L. Melvin III and he'd been acting in Ohio commercials since before the internet actually mattered. One of which was in a PSA commercial for foster-adoption. In it, Edward is a small hazel-eyed child searching for a home. In high school, Edward was a theater kid in Dayton, Ohio, before attending the University of Cincinnati for business marketing.

Eventually, Edward would join the internet and become Tré, and Tré wanted more for himself. At the time, the internet was fight videos and *WorldStarHipHop*. It made sense that his peers at the time were the likes of the rapper Freddy E., who would sadly pass in 2013, and the Viner Yung Poppy, who would receive a twelve-year prison sentence for selling a lethal dose of fentanyl to a victim.

In 2011, Black influencers were popping up overnight with their own sense of celebrity. Kid Fury's original YouTube presence was increasing his status in the Miami area. Other creators like Kingsley were cementing the culture and style of rapid-fire hot takes with his *Overexposed* series. After the nonpolitical, harsh comedy era of Wild'N Out and Yo Mama, internet comedians started framing themselves adjacent to their closest edge in the same way that Def Jam comedians did in the '90s. It's one of the beauties of time—like people—being many spokes on a wheel.

On October 9, 2011, while bored in a computer lab, Tré made his presence known on YouTube.

"I'd already uploaded my first video, 'Niggas These Days,'" Tré said over a Zoom call from New York. In an hour, he'd be going out with some friends. "I had already uploaded that to Facebook earlier that day, and all my friends and family were telling me to put it on You-Tube. I was like, okay, put it on YouTube and just kept ranting about shit that had me fucked up. And I think within a week, a week and four days, I had a thousand subscribers, and it just kept growing from there. But I guess the only thing I can remember is feeling activated, feeling activated, feeling invigorated, excited for what I definitely didn't see coming, what I didn't expect."[2]

The day Tré uploaded "Niggas These Days," I rode with some high school friends across Columbus to watch a fight at a park far away from the projects of the Hilltop. It's two strangers—a white boy from the wrestling team and someone I've only seen on my peripherals during walks through my cramped high school hallways. He might've been an athlete before the crumbling of our institutional access to sports, but now he only comes to school to dodge truancy and leaves as early as possible to pick up a duffle bag in his car and fade off into the city. I'm with my actual friends, but we're nosey.

In the back seat of the car, my chest reverberates. These speakers have bounce. They shake glass. They break fears. On another day, it's Chief Keef. Today, it's Waka Flocka Flame at the height of his career. The car is crammed with people, so the sound vibrates from shoulder to shoulder, quaking between ribs. It's the music of a berserker rage, contrasted by what's going on in the front seat: a scrawnier kid with a blunt between his lips cleaning the lens of his camera phone.

"Shit's gonna do numbers."

Our plan was to record the fight and post it. What happened was nothing of the sort. The fight wasn't too impressive, they went back and forth for some small amount of time before it became an outright wrestling match. The audience of the fight liked outright knockouts and brawling boxing. That audience is usually Black. But in Columbus our styles blend and spaces blur into something of a gray. I've learned the internet doesn't do gray. Success hinges on making something polarized in its context.

Two different fighting styles create a messy image in the end. The fight was over after less than two minutes, when the wrestler tried to shake his opponent's hand. We rolled our eyes, and our driver grumbled about the waste of gas. The kind of shit we liked was about building a frame of thought, a frame of mind. Keeping it up is just as utilitarian. Without it, the ambience asked for joy.

On our way back to our side of town, the scrawny kid put his phone on the dashboard. We were watching HotDamnIRock (72.K followers)—a YouTube comedian from the Midwest. He held our attention here and there. And, like most times, we inevitably found ourselves in a parking lot of a McDonald's. We talked about dating— the girls we've tried to ensnare. I simply smiled as they talked. They laughed at that: at my silence.

Tré Melvin's *This Is a Commentary* became something of a relic of its time, but it had a structure. Tré numbered almost all of his videos, creating an episodic feel to his channel. Where most channels operated by creating miniseries with their own angles, Tré designed his channel to be one extended season of a variety show. Sometimes, there would be skits. Sometimes, there would be talks. Most times, he targeted his audience—Black people. Mostly, Black teens. He captured the sense of Midwest style that was popular at the time. When the Cali-Swag movement moved through the country, a lot of it was Hollister and Abercrombie and Fitch bright neon colors and snapback hats. Men—and women—wore sleeved tattoos all the way down the length of our arms. But the kinds of men who pioneered an era like this, who stood at its head and sculpted its face, said things like "Dark-skinned women shouldn't wear red lipsticks" and perished gay men out of the line of sight and community.

Every one of Tré Melvin's early videos had an aesthetic to it. He rarely ever left the interior of that computer lab with its burgundy painted walls and a row of Apple computer screens.

When he first kicked off his career on YouTube, he was only nineteen. What is now a pathed career with many beaten footprints at the time was just a passing hobby for most of the people involved. However, it was a place for people to build their worlds. Walls and roofs and safe places to hide your thoughts and joy.

By the time I found *This Is a Commentary*, I was well into my junior year. I didn't know for sure if anyone else was watching. It felt calm. Tré's world was experimental compared to other creators at the time, likely inspired by the bend of the internet's humor along with the truth of his reality.

At first, one might not expect the success of other creators, but it is the unanimous agreement of the internet and this new era that there is an audience for just about everything. There is an audience for work that shouldn't exist in a fair world too.

He counts creators like Jenna Marbles, Shane Dawson, HotDamnIRock, Kingsley, and Jerry Levine as his inspirations, but, even then, there is something distant about the comedy he was doing. Black theater has always tried to do something distant from the theater that is popular for its time. It tries to never forget its base, to make characters that are a bit more familiar than they are not. Kingsley, an openly gay YouTuber, told his audience that contrary to popular belief that when it comes to the "It Gets Better" trend, it doesn't always.

In his iconic winter hat, he told his following about the many times as an out gay man well into his adulthood, homophobia still popped up. It isn't lost on me in this day how Kingsley was one of the few popular openly gay Black creators on the website. There is a word that the internet would eventually learn after an era where words like "feminism" were most poisoned: intersectionality. Feminist legal scholar Kimberlé Crenshaw once described intersectionality as the framework that has been used as a basis for translating "women's experience" and "the Black experience" into a unique perspective.[3]

While largely dealing with the issues Black women experience, it is also helpful for understanding a perspective of Black queerness.

In his video, Kingsley warns about the potential danger on the path of coming out. He warns his peers not to embellish the future too much, even when the danger they're facing is the patterns of self-harm that young queer kids experienced at the time.

I remember reading a comment when Kingsley posted the video. The person asked, that if being gay was so bad, why would he be openly gay on the internet. The irony of the question wasn't pointed out. It wasn't even answered. Because gay Black boys do not get the benefit of the doubt usually. When we are flamboyant or drive with a little too much sugar in the tank, we're clocked. There're a few levels of hiding we have to go through in order to properly fit in; not everyone can do it or wants to do it. When Kingsley entered the limelight, he smiled widely and didn't veil anything about who he was. His queerness, like his Blackness, was not up for censorship on his path to curating his space.

When Tré Melvin sat in front of the camera, there were aspects of the truth he considered not sharing himself. It's a question most creators ask themselves when they consider creating for the long haul, which is a way of saying you are bound to answering a calling, rather than answering a whim. And, as a man whose aspirations would eventually bring him to Juilliard for the most classical training as an actor, there were questions worth answering.

Blackness was not one of them.

In the beginning, Tré found that for most creators—not him—it was easier to either not identify as a "Black creator" or to simply choose not to be vocal about Black issues. The algorithm saw race as a redlined issue. It terminalized the success you could find with brands. In many cases, it still might. One could also find the reach to an audience who might be able to make use of the kinds of identities and conversations shortened at the joint.

This experience could be called a form of passing. Gaining traction—whether for the sake of credibility or profit—had the expectation of graying out parts of their Blackness best left unnoticed. This transmutation act should be difficult to perform because what is felt should not always have to be said to be real. But, in a would-be post-racial society, silence made transformation possible for creators who looked just like Tré Melvin.

What this silence caused is a string of philosophies on the role of the Black platform. An amateur perspective would be that Blackness is something that cannot be hidden. More provocative thinkers would say that one cannot be Black if one cannot tell they are Black. I don't engage in those topics. But, in this case, there are many ways for people to obscure Blackness. At least, obscure their dedication to it. One could lie about matters of the heart or ethics. One can become selfish in a culture of generosity. One can run from community and toward inclusion. One can be silent, creating a space of apolitical agenda that, in truth, becomes quite political.

Blackness, after all, is not just a skin color. It's the decorations for a space. It's a Watsonian painting of Black faces drinking whiskey and smoking cigarettes in a wooden shanty beneath two spotlights. It's Studio 54, where entrance for Black folk is not a suggestion but a requirement. It's a far distance from self-segregation and sits square in self-celebration.

Tré's content didn't ask questions or even apologize for what it was considering.

He had a series called *These Days*. It wasn't so much scrutiny, but his humor always bent toward different things he personally had problems with. Satire is hard. Tré made it look easy. Black people have a lot of hang-ups we must be aware of when we are making art. We don't always think about stock characters or themes, but we are aware of them. We don't want to caricature Black women, but when there are Black women who feel a way, whose lives go in a direction, that feels like a flowering in a wide garden that people thought would die, you can't help but sketch it again and again.

I didn't learn the word "ekphrasis" until I was in my master's program for writing. My professor called it "art about art." I realized that's my goal as a Black artist, because Blackness is an art form. It is about how we live our lives as much as it is about why. And the why is usually racism. But the how encompasses a thousand different cultural wheels moving independently of this singular blighted force. Poverty. Love. Dreams. Respect.

Tré collects some of this in his own way.

Eventually, Tré finds his way to his own femininity. However, the creator known as Tré Melvin won't come out of the closet until New Year's 2014. He does it in a video titled "My New Year's Resolution." It was a somber approach to his truth. Not many people like us practiced the habit of coming out publicly around then. It'd been almost a year since Frank Ocean came out the closet, and his exposure to the world was quite violent. At the time, influencers did not rock the boat or shake the tree when it came to their audience. It was a game of knowing what your kind of people wanted from you and serving it to them over and over again. But people aren't really idle like that. And artists are even less likely to be idle. The gift of creation belongs in the hands of people who seek spaces of newness—the blank canvas where charcoals draw color.

After Tré Melvin was publicly out, he wound up on a lot of Black blogs. Namely, Tré found himself the source of gossip on *WorldStar HipHop*, a hip-hop community gossip blog. *WorldStarHipHop* was known to me for two things: fight videos and the comments section. It is a relic of an old era of the internet before the violence of commentary could become a never-ending stream of conscious on apps like Instagram and TikTok.

As could be expected but not hoped for, the comments were merciless with Tré's coming out. They scrutinized his queerness not just from a religious standpoint but a racial and entertainment one. He wasn't just a gay creator. He was emblematic of a deep-seated corruption in the arts turning Black men weak.

Eventually, Tré sent the staff of *WorldStarHipHop* a message, for his own well-being. While *WorldStarHipHop*'s commentary was known to be exacting and merciless, it seemed the team behind the website were not. They took the video down despite the views they received from it.

Ironically, Tré regretted asking for mercy.

"When I look back at that, I'm like, 'Oh, I wish I hadn't done that. Fuck that. Fuck them.' I mean, how does faggot hurt you once you've accepted it?"

It's a developed inclination. One that requires a question of what your queerness means in relationship with your connection to the online atmosphere. Many creators have asked if they're allowed to be offended by comments made by people whose idea of them has been cultivated by an algorithm. Many Black people of a certain background cracked by hardship have asked if receiving mercy is an admission of weakness. I grew up having "riff sessions" on the front stoop, mercilessly mocking people whose names I say with love now. I told myself if they asked me to stop, I would. I know they would never ask me to stop. I know they'd never admit to feeling owed their soft spots salved.

I bring this into adulthood as a Black queer man. I haven't stopped being quick with my words. I have become more willing to ask to be salved. I tried to be like lightning to my fellow man, like the cold fire in the skies that happens from time to time.

By the end of his coming-out video, Tré lands on a path toward acceptance. He has to. Tré will navigate Black queerness in the public eye and thus if he cannot accept himself, he risks being defined by what others interpret about him through his work. His art reflected this newness, too, at the axis where a queer content creator's work differed from the straight gaze.

But before this happens he wanders an ancient library of what the industry could call controlled repression. Their labels and genres are optional, but they are also not. Because the idea you have to redefine yourself to succeed is the grand design of oppression. What is acceptable—and unchanged—is what is normal. What is normal is what the empire's voice serves. If Black queer artists could feel normal, so much of our art would not thrive in the gutter's dark. So much of Black queer art would not feel alien to both gutters of the Black and the queer. So much of what completes our community's truth would not need to be called scandalous for its basic miracle of reflection.

Tupac once had a lot to say about a rose growing through the concrete. Tupac ought to have said something about the rainbows in the storm—the shining colors that break the swirling dark and wet. The bitter stink of sulfur eroding the exhilarating notes of sugar. It is a challenge of intimacy among a hall of barbs and needles.

BETTER A PERFORMER THAN A PRODUCT

That same year, 2015, a Charleston, South Carolina, parishioners met for a bible study at the Emanuel African Methodist Episcopal Church. The church is a historic landmark. For centuries, Black mothers and Black children have called it a space of sanctity and safety. It was the first independent Black denomination, where our Blackness found the long-neglected roots of Christianity.

This location has an unprecedented religious origin. One of its founders, Denmark Vesey, was implicated in a slave uprising plot. He was swiftly convicted in a kangaroo court and lynched within a month. The substance of his trial was a secret, though multiple other trials followed Vesey's lynching. More than thirty souls were dismissed from the flesh and heat of the Earth. Others were deported, including Vesey's son. The original Emanuel AME Church was burned down by an angry mob of white people, one of the more dangerous elements of American society in any age. The congregation fled to the underground of South Carolina.

Another cofounder was imprisoned for months without a crime. When he was released, he and others fled to Philadelphia and established a new life there among the booming Black communities of the North. Following this, Nat Turner's slave rebellion kicked off in 1831 and Charleston outlawed all-Black churches entirely. During this period of faithlessness, Charleston became a hub of supernatural curiosity. One such curiosity was John Domingo, reportedly the most powerful conjure-man in South Carolina. He was known as the Black Constable, and the neighborhood respected his powers as law. Many feared him as a Union soldier because of the greatcoat he wore, with his lion's mane hair down his shoulders. Others speculated that he was High John de Conquer, an African prince, and used his African powers gifted to him by his birthright as a noble blood to charm emancipation and bespelling Erzuli herself into love.

It was legend that his love spells and healing enchantments were unparalleled—as were his gifts to distort the weather. And his enemies regarded his dark side as a necromancer, capable of raising the dead and filling households with the souls of their most wronged by slavery. Many white citizens of Charleston feared him, but his one weakness was the power and worship of Jesus. Some say he blasphemed Jesus and his powers turned on him there on a street after he was called to conjure against a pair of thieves. In any case, his death substantiated the power of God and the necessity of faith in his Christian powers to steer away the potential of other haints and supernatural curiosities.

The church would eventually resurface sometime after the Civil War. The white majority of South Carolina had tried to spook it into submission with violence, lynchings, and death and failed. And the state learned that the absence of faith institutions is not an absence of terror.

While the digital world has denounced Christianity as a white man's religion, the roots of this Southern church was a reminder to the many new ways Black Americans have invested our indigenous spirituality into the practice and resurfaced the old Colored roots of Christian worship. The carnal power of a fetish and those anointed through story to dictate the honors and guidance of our community—that old Negro craft as close to the earth as mud. Through churches and faith as Black as these, we find exactly how Black people breathed spirit into the Word of God. Such is a space that denounces that a slave ought to bow to their master. Such is a space that preaches the flames in the spirit of the Jewish as they stood with Moses against the Pharaoh. Such is the image of old African left hands slinged in war against false idols, like the idols worshipped by the racism of Jim Crow.

Dylann Roof, a white supremacist, marched into the halls of Emanuel African Methodist Episcopal Church with a flame-like steel and murdered nine people in a spree. Nine people with a firearm. One survived with memory of the heat within a bullet, with the experience to pass on what it means to survive, what hate feels like, and how it feels to be shot.

As blood clung together pages on bibles as sacred as this murderer thought his duty, the world watched as police brought Dylann Roof into a jail cell alive. We remember the many Black men and women who would never have that chance. We say their names in electric letters so their power might be felt.

A month later, a Black woman is found hanging in a Texas jail cell. Her picture upon detainment is notably discolored and strange. People speculate if she was actually alive when her picture was taken.

She, too, we remember. We say her name in electric letters, but we do not call for peace this time. We call for power. And we wait for the powerful to abide. Tré Melvin was among those who answered first and without hesitation:

A lot of Black creators, specifically Black queer creators who began speaking out again just on our issues, found themselves pushed less to their subscribers, to the public in general. And this is not even just with YouTube, this is across a lot of different platforms. I remember there was a time when, I want to say when Black Lives Matter really, really started gaining notoriety and I was opening my big-ass mouth speaking and I remember there was a time where my account wouldn't even show up if you search "Tré Melvin" on Instagram. It was some good blacklistings, some good shadow-banning anger.[4]

Blacklisting and bans are dangerous for artists in this arts era. Most income is tethered to the ad revenue we accrue over a library of content. If we are being suppressed by the algorithm, as many Black creators are, that is one thing. However, being unable to be found by our audiences with the help of the search engine, that's a different problem. Most content creators post across a rainbow of apps to entice interest in a process most call "cross-pollination," or they manually lure audiences from one platform to join another. This is a process that would eventually come to dominate with the arrival of Patreon and the ability to turn one viewer into a dollar of profit. Thus, if only 12 percent of one's following contributed a dollar after you got into the YouTube Creator Program, one would have more than enough income to fund other creative pursuits without a day job. The violence of suppression for speaking on Black issues and the atrocities of police brutality was punitive.

"I was pissed," said Melvin.

I was angry. But it also pushed me to either take necessary steps back from creating and just focus on myself and my mental or create platforms outside of it. In 2020, when I left YouTube after George Floyd was murdered and I spoke out on it and they demonetized me, it was just the perfect time because I had already been speaking to my late best friend, Kathy, rest in peace, since February that year. I had already been speaking to her about a spirit pushing me to leave YouTube and I'd already started fleshing out my own streaming service, my own platform, *Tré Melvin TV*. And that was really just the last straw after they killed George. So, yeah, it pushed me to create my own shit, to build my own shit.

The slowed traction for Tré limited progress only a bit, but it did not entirely. The lesson in the absence of his space and power after this moment was quite tangibly what happens to Black creators who rely solely on outside instruments. Sure, now YouTube might claim to support Black lives and creators; however, what is now realized is how much of this support depends on the vogue of the stakes at hand. And while digital space allows one to create from anywhere in the world with an internet connection, it does not always allow the diversification of profit when it comes to living as an artist. If you—if Tré—wanted to keep his mission established so clearly now of supporting Black lives and himself, he'd have to make moves to position power squarely in his hands.

By the end of 2015, with an insanely popular character in tow, Tré Melvin would follow in the footsteps of many YouTube creators before him and move to Los Angeles, where collaboration and opportunity abound more prevalently. Most YouTube creators in Hollywood often found hurdles with translating their success online into other tangible opportunities.

Tré describes his average day in 2015 as mostly a party. So, he summarized his life the same way with brief captions under filtered pictures on Instagram and Twitter. Some drinking in West Hollywood. Fucking up a dance floor. Not a lot of work in the gym, despite the expectation of what beauty has to behave like living above Compton. In Los Angeles—at least the parts mired by recent community erected as hastily as those who arrived left their homes—social popularity can become a daily culture. Not many people recognized the work that became Tré's life when he wasn't sharing this image, because it was not the parts of what he was doing some might believe him capable of doing.

To many, Tré became Hollywood, rather than the artist he sustained in practice: writing, filming, and editing behind the scenes. The long sharpening an artist takes to refine the stories they will tell about those small hours spent upkeeping craft. Audiences did not feel the ache in your fingers after long hours typing or the wary estimation of energy three hours after bedtime or five hours after bed time or the time when the sun breaks through blackout shades and tells you it is too late to snatch a couple hours of sleep.

The artist alchemy of time that renders masterpiece.

Going Hollywood has always been synonymous with the way rubbing shoulders with the existing empire and institution can taint the nature of one's preexisting work. In truth, this can happen. Formerly progressive and radical minds suddenly become supportive of the systems that once held a gun to their head. Activists turned entourage turned models and salesmen after just a few years of proximity to celebrity engagements. However, what slowly developed over the course of Melvin's time online—and the death of apps like Vine and Tumblr—included the resurgence of conversations that were once disproved. Namely, questioning the nature of his character of Watermelondrea Jones and if her existence is synonymous with harm.

> I battled that [harm conversation] at the beginning of [my spiritual] shift, and during the shift, and people would make comments about that, and make sure . . . like I said, I just wanted to be sure at the end of the day . . . I was going to kill her off a while ago to appease everybody. And that was a really long, really hard battle for me.

I just remember coming to the conclusion after speaking with the Black woman about her, the Black women in my life about her, that people are just . . . they're always going to find an issue. And as long as my intentions are good, at the end of the day, that's really all that fucking matters. And as long as I can keep using her to speak real shit that people won't . . . they're not going to listen to me say, they're not going to go to the library and read no book about it. As long as I can keep using her to heal and to shift narratives and all that shit, then I'm going to do it. But it took me a minute to come to that conclusion. And I know a lot of it also was just really rooted in the homo-fucking-phobia.

A faint hum of spirituality followed the new era of Tré Melvin: of questions and answers of purpose and practice. *This Is a Commentary* was gone and it was all the man beneath the wig at work. And some work isn't just on a page or a platform.

And then, Tré killed himself.

Not really.

In 2022, Tré Melvin posted an obituary for himself, after the tragic death of his best friend, Kathy Pacheco-Mendoza, in a car accident that Tré survived with significant brain injury. It impacted his journey. It impacted his path. Online, a particularly cruel sect of trolls accused Tré of sacrificing loved ones in a ritual sacrifice. This isn't a rare conspiracy theory; however, most who endure it are not private citizens.

To mark his return to the public, but also to shed the life he was living before his spiritual shift, Tré posted his obituary. A black-and-white portrait on a navy backdrop. "In Loving Memory of Tré Melvin: October 28th, 1992–May 6th, 2022."

It's been a year since my quote unquote death hoax from last year where everybody ate me up on the internet. I know people thought like, "Ooh, we getting under his skin. Oh, we got to . . ." And the gag is: first of all, this was planned. It was planned. It was coordinated very well. It was the longest break I've taken from social media, and the only thing I knew—between the tweets and the Facebook posts and the news articles and shit—the only thing I knew was shit that my team was sending me, if I wanted to hear it.

But I really had them focus on sending the positives, because it gets so easy to fall into the negatives on the internet. But it was one of the most freeing moments for me, because it wasn't what everyone made it out to be. It was so much deeper to me. It wasn't for views, it wasn't for promotion, it wasn't any of that. It was actually a very big spiritual shift for me, and I wanted to share that with people, and I knew it would people off, which is why we prepared.

Following his spiritual shift, Tré Melvin pulled down the space around him that he'd cultivated: more so than when he came out, because in that era Blackness on the internet had stipulations, it had rules, it had guidelines of respectability and who could profit and so many at the nip of a single platform that had only so much attention to give out. What he created in its stead was calibrated.

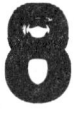

Know where you come from
to know who you are.

—A BLACK TEACHER

REMEMBER MEME IRL

Let's do a throwback real quick.

Race and politics have never been foreign concepts to the internet. The digital space has almost always been preoccupied with the nature of the outside world. This preoccupation is performed by pushing to transcend the confines and biases of the real world—creating a heaven on magical flat-screens by any means necessary. Or by obsessively clinging to their inherited power in our real world through verbal and spiritual abuse against Black and Brown people on the blissful neutrality of the internet. But these are extremes. From what can be accounted for on the internet, both Black identity and our pain are never simply one or the other but a sticky-smooth blend. Our pain is parodied, but it can only be so hysterical because the audience gets our truth after so many times that Black folk have communicated it. Empathy is not always guaranteed in this blend, though. For empathy, what is communicated about Black folks' truth would eventually arrive at *understanding*.

I first came across the culture of memes absent-mindedly, when in my sophomore-year Accelerated English course, as a writing project, we created our own blogs. It was 2010 and the course only existed because Franklin Heights High School wouldn't yet approve of sophomores taking AP classes. Yet we couldn't be in ordinary classes either. Our school thought it would be dangerous to mix "gifted" students with our fine GPAs into the general population of the school. It was something of a mystery, why not. This separation bred an insulated culture separate from the issues of the wider class. When I was in the hallways, I was the younger brother of Alexis, a cooler type of girl who was friends with just about everyone and had every willingness to remind people that they came second to blood save those whom she loved like blood. The hallways cared about athletics, which is something we nearly lost when the South Western School District cut all transportation options, extracurriculars, and our AP course work after a levy for funds to be built with a minor increase in taxes (just the amount of a two-liter soda every week) failed.

In 2008, the district cut $10.9 million from school year spending, putting everyone at risk—coaches, bus drivers, club leaders, conductors, band coordinators, extracurricular educators, and more. Before this, I committed to being more popular on a bet with my sister, who said I couldn't do it: that I just didn't have something resembling likability. She called me lame because in truth, I was a square. I said it was easier than she thought to be like everyone else.

And so I did it. It took a while, but by the end, I had as many friends as she did—though I couldn't say if they liked me—and most of the work was just joining social media. All you needed was an email address and a willingness to endure the psychological humiliation involved with online judgment for tastes and points of view. Watch the right shows (*Degrassi* and *I Love New York*) react to the right songs (Lil Wayne on *LimeWire* and obscure battle rappers fresh out of Philly) and learn the right dances—Crank Dat, Bird Walk, and the Reject. I might have singular kinks in my grand design—being bisexual and sometimes showing that when I rambled a little too long about how good Nicki Minaj was—but, overall, I could average a C grade in my accomplishments. I passed for a year at least and my position wasn't going to *pretend* to last against the sports culture of high school . . . until the levee broke and ruined it.

A woman named Rachel wrote that as a concerned citizen out of high school, our student council should write a letter to our PTA presidents, athletic boosters, and music booster presidents. They said we should reach out to local parent groups. She pushed for all of us to fight against the silence by forcing noise in the homes of every member of our city hellbent on erasing our futures.

Just a few months after an amendment passed returning extracurriculars once a string of car accidents involving pedestrian students and a considerable uptick in teen crimes occurred, the school—both faculty and student body—were quite keen on rebuilding the once legendary reputation of our athletics department. In Columbus, Ohio, financial aid is something of a white hen. As far back as I can remember in Ohio schooling, we were reminded of the expenses necessary to attend college anywhere. We knew of loans, but many of us were not promised them. We knew of academic scholarships, but those were offered only to the cream of the graduating crop and were also highly competitive. This left two final options in the Buckeye State: the US military and athletic scholarships. These were the differences between flipping burgers, hard manual labor, and the gilded gates of academia.

Athletics would never be it for me. Sports culture in Ohio was such a pasttime that we were shocked as a collective that the levy failed in the first place because it'd put an end to the high school athletics season entirely. No one program was impacted by this decision: not the theater, not just arts and clubs, not just student government, but anything that didn't involve showing up to class and raising a hand in a sea of twenty-five other hands. I know parents who kept their kids generally participating in every sport year-round just to increase their likeliness that eventually one pastime will be lucrative enough for that eventual pivot.

Even on the north side of Columbus, I had friends and cousins tied up in Pee-Wee and Little League sports. My cousin dated boys who all knew each other from the never-ending parade of scrimmages and training camps. They added each other on MySpace and eventually they added each other on Facebook. They maintained contact in group chats and message boards. They played Halo and eventually 2K's varying forms together online. When a girl who might've been on the intramural cheerleading and spirit teams stepped to one of them, changed her mind, and stepped to another of them, they compared notes to one another, careful not to break up whatever fragile fraternity was going on—or threw the fresh energy of a new rivalry into their next game (or on the streets, whichever came first). Mothers created support groups with recommendations for bulk snack purchasing, effective brands for those deep Ohio colds and carpooling schedules; present fathers made highlight reels for YouTube and compared notes on potential D-1 candidates using statboards posted to hastily prepared blog sites and websites.

These interlinking networks of relationships would eventually come in handy summer of 2020, when news of flash protests had to circulate through Columbus, and civilians—white and Black—had to coordinate in power in front of a city executive branch that now worked against its people not just in private city council meetings, but actively with the US president and the National Guard.

These were athletes. Maybe 70 percent of the schools between varsity and junior varsity. Likewise, it hadn't yet been expected that every household had a single desktop computer, let alone a laptop for every person indoors. Smartphones weren't a standard. Particularly not the iPhone, which had just thrust itself out of the pockets of the hipster culture but were still not approachable for average teens. "I don't ever expect a teenager to have an iPhone. I see one of those, I know you got money," said my high school government teacher.

However, when the levy failed, everyone was pushed to go digital. This was a political push. We needed to have a place to centralize our voice and strategize against the realistic selfishness of our community. It might be at most two dollars every week to keep our sports going in our district, but two dollars is not what our opposition made of it. Online, we created a page to centralize our campaign: to gather our power and plans for the community.

The battle was uphill. Through Facebook, we had an open portal into the minds and feelings of our community. Those without kids thought that school should be for education. They said that if we did not have extracurriculars as a distraction, we could excel more academically. What we did outside of homework and tests to them were frivolous to our overall development. Worse, in Ohio a growing culture of anti-intellectualism contributed not only to the dominant sports culture, but to the myth that school is the place where children go to be tempted by "deviant philosophies" like identity, race, and sexuality. The South Western City School District overlapped several neighborhoods that transformed the schools in this district into melting pots of culture. Judaism and Islam laid their crown at desks beside Christianity. Black and white commingled. Somali and Ethiopian learned the tongues of American culture. White students were amazed when their friends would vanish from the halls to fast over the holiday of Ramadan. During the earliest iterations of Soulja Boi and the Crank Dat dance crazes, when most teens over the summer of 2007 were learning the choreography to over twenty different Crank Dat performances, like TikTok kids in Gen Alpha, white students were apprehensive about cementing themselves in public displays of Blackness at home. A few friends voiced that the only time they ever had an opportunity to learn was during summer sports and clubs or outside in the neighborhood with their friends. The issue with this at time was due to the online and user-generated nature of the movement, by the time one dance could be mastered, two more popped into existence. If you weren't with it as fast as possible, you missed out. It would be two years before Soulja Boi cemented his version of the trend in the single "Crank Dat (Soulja Boi)," which propelled him as one of the first Black content creators among superstardom. It was largely propelled by his accent, truthfully. Atlanta rappers started breaking the crust out of the crunk era of hard production and club bangers that went up *only* in the clubs. Club music, being a certain kind of acoustic—the kind adjusted by professional DJs in front of expensive equipment and speaker systems that could handle a lot of bass where home equipment, like one-dollar headphones from the dollar tree or microspeakers, burst under at a certain decibel.

As its existing talents faded out and returned to the South to build the baronies of the country grammar, new Atlanta sounds came out swinging tying tone to the East Coast rap style. Prominently, these rappers created music that could be played anywhere. Soulja Boi especially made music that was the sound of the millennial generation— for dance crazes, loverboy antics, and viral videos. Traditional rappers hated it, so our parents did too. And, thus, kids loved him more.

While the voters of Columbus could be extremely racist and xenophobic, there was cause for the gradual cultural shifts going on. Overnight, cornhole-loving kids would divest from the culture that made their households great and bring home subtle, slight demands that alienated the histories of their families. This was because for every white student starting on a sports team, there were ten others who were not white. And these students, surrounded by a dominant culture that did not center white expressionism and in fact actively rejected it, would attempt to adopt as much Blackness as possible by osmosis. The internet contributed to this cycle more as social feeds became flooded by local impressions of quality music.

In 2007, Kanye West dropped his third studio album, *Graduation*. To drum up sales and marketing, West scheduled his release on the same day as 50 Cent's *Curtis*. It became a friendly competition, but also a major online debate. It was perhaps my first experience with an online trend. Unlike earlier trends with the Crank Dat dance, our white classmates had to demand access to the Black channels in order to measure the success of their allegiance. By the time Kanye West won the contest by outselling 50 Cent by an overwhelming margin, BET was banned from the homes of half of our white student body. They couldn't demand a segregation of schools during an early Obama-era presidency. However, by the time the levy hit in 2009, there was little to no hope for the continued cross-pollination anywhere—

Except the digital world.

Eventually, competitive fathers watched as their sons were pushed off local athletic clubs and teams in favor of kids with much more efficient overall scores on ranking sites. In the past, they had the benefit of the doubt through in-person performance. Now, coaches were going out of their way to manipulate anything down to addresses to recruit teens. Black athletes held the large majority of the social capital at the school and typically traded their hands at as diverse a dating pool as possible, further concerning local white fathers and mothers.

Ohio might hold its symbol of the buckeye as close to its heart as possible, but it was extremely wary of the poison it allowed its kids to consume.

When the levy's supporters campaigned, our educators managed door-to-door, pavement-pounding advocacy. Many kids who didn't have a Facebook account made one. One concerned citizen named Rachel stepped up in the Student Campaign Group. She invoked the name of the student council to pen letters to PTA presidents. Make an impatient plea to local parent groups. To take up space in the July parades and midsummer festival seasons. There were plenty of public parks to dominate with our pleas, our needs, our worth.

But we were kids. Barely out of middle school and shy about the nature of honest emotion or what these programs meant to us as people too poor to change districts once this all went sour (as our wealthier friends did). We had to ask for a ride to the skating rink and the movie theaters. And we didn't know how to send letters to all of these people in such a short amount of time when they'd just as easily be thrown away or stomach phone calls that got ignored.

By the time we finally passed the levy after a second failure, the accelerated students had already formed a similar understanding to their parents. School was for learning, not sports. However, the funding for our future depended on more than learning—our merit would never be enough for as long as we were poor. The community seemed to forget that. This bred an insular us-versus-them mentality that was extremely hard to shake. And the student handbook validated that by tracking us in different demands for graduation. On one side of the school was a program built for the athletes, the track that had smaller stipulations for achievement but an overwhelming focus of our administration, and on the other side was the AP kids in the college track, which required extracurriculars, foreign languages, and more to prepare us for college. Of course, we all had to pass the Ohio Graduation Test, but it was expected that no one in the college track would ever struggle. Some of us didn't. I didn't. Regardless, it bred contempt, and that contempt became the basis of other, problematic points of view. There were only three of us among that crowd who didn't entirely fit into these dynamics either.

I was not the only Black kid in the class. I know it is the vogue to suggest this overall, but I grew up in a period of time where some stereotypes were not the norm, which made things like microaggressions and racism substantially harder to point out. There were a few of us. However, many of them were athletes—track and basketball, mostly—and many of them were more competitive for their academic acumen than their athletics. I felt the sting largely as a student from a single-parent household from one of the local Section 8 housing complexes. My intelligence was not the mark of ambition like theirs, but simply a desire to understand. I didn't always do my homework, because I was uninterested in *proving* how much I knew on a paper rather than showcasing it in class.

By the end of my high school career, I was nowhere near the competition for the highest GPA in our class, averaging a 2.2 through high testing and low assignment completion. Their opinion of me was that I was not smart enough to be in the room with them. Half of them called me the "Black Rousseau" on account that I would only occasionally have a romantic, useful insight that could muster into much of anything. Sometimes. Only sometimes.

Perhaps it was easier to tackle me in this way. I was closer to the world that they'd grown to disdain. How often did the community rally to the protection of the student band ecosystem that our Accelerated program took pride in? The band, after all, had connections to D-1 schools as well. All of our students had on some level supported the "Best Damn Band in the Land" on a weekly basis, running concessions for Ohio State and more, but they were almost entirely absent from conversations.

I was not in band because instruments cost the kind of money that my mother could not spare. I felt no comfort in sports, because my body felt ruptured with any overactive stimulation—an early sign of what my mother would learn is Ehlers-Danlos syndrome, a neuromuscular disease that gapes the joints, softens the skin, and depletes the body's ability to retain active energy levels. Most of my adolescence was instead spent propped up in front of a computer screen. I was sometimes an online gamer: not a great one, just sometimes. *Habbo Hotel* and *Gaia Online*, with the occasional penchant for 2D flash games like *Runescape*, *Adventure Quest*, and *Dragon Fable*. I liked roleplay servers. It beheld a majesty for conversation and story. I didn't wear bright colors. I didn't wear colors at all—just dulled grays and blacks to create a personality so neutral I could flow wherever I needed to fit in. I didn't create a thing, not even a ripple in the ocean of our student body.

When the levy failed and sports dominance of the school was shattered, the Accelerated students found their own sense of power as the outsiders. On the blogosphere, where we performed our class-work, we created our own little ways to sneak past the watchful eye of our teacher, who was coming for grammar and ideas rather than understanding and translating. Throughout the smaller paragraphs, in itty bitty lines there were references to a sputtering philosopher in the name of the Black Rousseau.

It was my first meme.

WHAT IT IS, WHAT IT MEMES

Digital Black art runs on memes. They are little snapshots into moments, ideas, and feelings that you only get if you are in the know. It's how I became most familiar with the daily reality of code-switching in the light of day. Changing out of my formal language to speak to a community that could feel the heartbeat of my cultural emotion.

They are also currency. Proof of your legitimacy in the world. Recognizing even one makes you a curator. And once Twitter created the culture of the reaction video, a video clip played to season a reply to another person, it turned curators into collectors.

When Vine was at its apex, the language of the internet, too, was formed. Thickened tongue constricted around shapes and sounds that had a spirituality to it. Naturally, Black creators became the center of the gaze: sometimes quite apathetically.

Tay Zonday's "Chocolate Rain" was widely memed everywhere, turned into an interjection across the digital landscape. Never mind that "Chocolate Rain" was a song detailing the crushing perspective that race politics envelop Black people with. The Blackness of it all could be cast aside like pistachio shells for the digestible flavor of mockery.

Tay Zonday's lyrics speak of a grief inherited from a father: Blackness. It speaks of the self-blinding of a Black boy to the reality of his harm, a microcosm where one can protect one's own perception. It asks the question of if it is better to ignore the daily aggressions to feed the illusion that none of it actually touches you or is it better to simply ignore the outside of the tent. Like most art on Blackness, it doesn't pretend to not have the answers. There is a condemnation to whatever they are doing, but it is still an awareness that there is a choice to be made.

There's something about the despair of Blackness that speaks to the internet's fantasies. Perhaps it has something to do with the juxtaposition: Black men are pressed into molds all the time. Typically, they are hard, cold, and molten like tar, crumbling only with never-ending friction. However, I've often noted and twote that Black men are most emulated when we are at our most feminine. Cam'ron in a pink fur coat is perhaps the most meme'd moment of the mid-aughts despite how the reality of this image is suggested to drive the supposed emasculation of the Black man in the wider media (what isn't in this day and age, according to digital misogynists).

July 28, 2010: Antoine Dodson concluded an interview with Elizabeth Gentle, a reporter. Standing in a red bandanna, fresh tears on his black hoodie, in front of the Lincoln Park housing project in Huntsville, Alabama, Antoine's voice touched the world:

> Well, obviously we have a rapist in Lincoln Park. He's climbin' in yo windows, he's snatchin' yo people up, tryin' to rape 'em. So y'all need to hide yo kids, hide yo wife, and hide yo husband cause they rapin' err'body out here.[1]

Immediately, there were attacks on Dodson's slang. They said he didn't make the Black community look good. Members of the Huntsville, Alabama, community suggested that Dodson made their town look bad to the world. Dodson's own sister suggested that he turn away from media attention because the video made him look like a fool.

They suggested that the video reinforced stereotypes, never mind that not only was Dodson a *real* person speaking in his *real* way, that the circumstances were entirely real to him and the victim he was speaking for. *The Grio* made a slideshow labeled "The Most Ignorant Viral Videos of All Time" and included the video. There was a comments section on websites like *WorldStarHipHop* that suggested censorship, largely because of Dodson's visibly queer mannerism. They didn't want Dodson to exist, to be real. Dodson had champions, too, but not in the way one might hope. In this sect, the Gregory Brothers saw a goldmine. They made a song called "The Bed Intruder Song" by remixing the audio and video of his interview. You can barely recognize the desperation in his face. Even I fell for the flattened humor of the remix. The song made it to number eighty-nine on *Billboard*'s Hot 100 list.

Rather than get angry, Dodson instead demanded a cut of the profits for the viral hit, along with ownership of his own intellectual property. He created his own website. The Black man hustled for the single-minded goal of removing his family from the environment that would not only allow his sister to be victimized but mocked it. I understand the sentiment. A community that would raise its flags at the fact a gay Black man from the hood spoke instead of the real rapist running free.

Dodson launched a campaign to raise money to get his family up out the ghetto. In August 2010, Dodson, in a very much Lisa Left-Eye fashion, laughed at the irony of poverty while having an iTunes hit. In just a month of hustle, he moved his family out of the projects. He launched a merchandise line, a Halloween costume, a sex offender tracking device for iPhone and Android. He made a pilot episode for a reality TV show (never picked up). By 2022, Dodson made plans to launch a beer line. Behind the scenes, Dodson had already attended Virginia College and gotten an associate's degree in business administration. He'd been quite vocal about his experiences as a victim of rape in the past.

Dodson has since had a son. Tyler Perry cast him in *A Madea Christmas*. He dabbled as a Hotep, complete with homophobia and insinuations that he would support his child if he was gay—granted if he couldn't be "fixed." He participated in a subsequent apology video, one of the first of its genre. And he has officially declared himself a card-carrying bisexual.

It would be years before I would find out if the intruder alleged to have tried raping Antoine Dodson's sister was ever captured. Rashaad Cooper, the alleged intruder, was never tried. However, they both competed in a "celebrity" boxing match, where Dodson beat him squarely in a single round. Cooper broke his ankle in the ring and had to be carried out. Tragic.

What the source of this issue reveals—regardless of Dodson's own entrepreneurial spirit with his content or whether or not he felt okay with a painful moment being commodified—is that the internet has a fascination with not just Black pain but with discarding Black authenticity. It is flippant in its antics with this.

Regardless, what Dodson established would be the scaffolding for viral stardom. Dodson established that online stardom through content could be profitable if you were willing to be fodder for their rage. And this violence gave voice and agency to the people of the internet who weren't afraid of showing their ass.

Though Dodson was not the only Black meme turned mockery.

///////////

The year 2008 was not an especially eventful period in American history—if you can ignore Barack Obama's "Yes We Can" campaign, Beyoncé's *I Am . . . Sasha Fierce,* and Lil Wayne dropping *The Carter III.* Most of the country felt like a wasteland. Pennies were pinched tighter than an icy cold tension. A fugue of gray covered most matters. Life felt longer than it needed to be, seconds flooding a household.

In this gray that lasts so long you can feel it piling on your skin as heavy as snow.

In 2008, Scarlet was singing an original song in a room alone as her grainy webcam recorded. She wore a black blouse and jeans. The entire scene is smudged because of the camera quality—but you can make out the vague shapes of a college dorm. She climbed onto a simple wooden coffee table in the middle of her performance. That table collapsed and history was made when Scarlet took a tumble.

What started as an ordinary singing video from Scarlet turned into a worldwide laugh as Scarlet fell from a coffee-table-turned-stage for a performance while playing hooky from school. As shared on *The Jennifer Hudson Show,* Scarlet uploaded the video to YouTube in order to share the link with her sister. Over the course of the long wait, she forgot to set it to private. When she returned later, Scarlet saw the video had been public for some time. Rather than worry, Scarlet ignored the video.

It was an early viral hit from then on. Scarlet's real name might be Paige Reynolds, but she became immortalized as "Scarlet Takes a Tumble." That video was uploaded, deleted, and then reuploaded so many times the copies of the copies could no longer be recognized.

Thousands made reaction videos and shared them with their friends and followers. YouTuber Shane Dawson (19.1 million You-Tube subscribers) made a reaction with a stuffed animal. After an appearance on the Comedy Central digital clip show *Tosh.o,* Scarlet went offline. She'd go to college and become an RA. She'd get a degree in psychology. She'd become a therapist and dedicate herself to helping others. The video would not go away. Scarlet was haunted by it. It was one of the many staples connecting the early era of viral stardom: when no one knew what could happen from becoming a meme.

Today, Scarlet considers the viral hit a blessing.

In the early days of Vine, Black users stood out when they were participating in the app. Some comedians worked on their brands and their relationship with the algorithm with strategy and intention, just to be undercut with one moment—one singular spark where a creator did something, typically embarrassing.

///////////

In the 2011/12 school year, our Accelerated program graduated into a series of AP courses with many of the same faces. We did not disengage from the use of technology in the classroom. Twice a week we were at our computers, using proxy servers to get on to gaming and social media sites. Twitter had reached popularity, and most of us—if not all of us—had procured a smartphone of some sort. My first one was an Android, but I also was given an iPod Touch for Christmas with access to a cache of apps exclusive to iOS like the then-Apple-exclusive app Instagram.

In an increasingly digital era, the faculty began to center more digitally creative pursuits for the students. During the 2009 stint, this manifested with a pivot to the morning news teams for Franklin Heights High School. With the rise of YouTubers and influencer marketing, our senior class designed a new angle to the program that decentered "serious" journalism and instead leaned into comedy skits that targeted our student body. The creator of this program was not Black, but a white kid most folk only described as "down."

Adam Little would go on to become a comedian, writer, and content creator prominent on YouTube. Back then, he started a series of comedy skits taking full advantage of the digital equipment and editing software in the morning news program. See, our teachers used grants and budgeting to procure not only digital cameras with SD cards and functioning microphones, but Mac computers fully equipped with the editing software. Naturally, he used the equipment to make his own comedy shorts—all with an apparent Andy Samberg Lonely Island approach. He also looped in remarkable Black students from our school with a myriad of creative talents.

One of them, MarShawn McCarrel, was a deeply empathetic spirit who had a penchant for freestyle and slam poetry. He frequented cafés and poetry nights all around Columbus. Once, during a homecoming game, when his brother and his friends were throwing things at me—and not just me but my friends—I leapt up out of my seat fully prepared to fight. It is one of my more defiant moments, as my friends recalled. They knew me to be one of the more levelheaded individuals, slower to anger or violence. They didn't understand the difference between a bully and a friend even with how niggas blur the lines.

MarShawn squared the issue. He apologized for his brother. He humbled himself for his brother. And, in turn, his brother apologized. I thought it was simply the balancing act siblings make, where either pushes or pulls on one another's flaws and favors. I'd come to know this as MarShawn's nature. He had a butterscotch personality, a mellow sweetness that held firm until it mattered. He made mixtapes that interrogated as much as they empathized. MarShawn did the sorts of things that made you want to follow in his footsteps. With his "Feed the Streets" food drive program, he didn't win the 2016 NAACP Hometown Hero Award, but he embodied it and, thus, it always belonged to him.

I always talked to MarShawn with respect and he to me whenever we passed in the halls. He'd later become a prominent hometown activist in Columbus, working against the city's legislative assaults against the poor, the unhoused, and the Black at the alleged beckoning of big corporations like Walmart.

But at this time, he was with Adam Little in almost every single skit. Adam off-the-screen discussed adverse censorship from the faculty who saw digital content creation and shorts as limited, another sign of the shortsightedness of us teenagers. When Adam started posting the morning news skits to his YouTube account and social media after the premiere on our school TV sets, they warned of his digital footprint.

One teacher complained, "You'll pop up in job searches in the future. Then what will you say? Your dumb decisions as a kid will impact you later. Watch."

They didn't say this to Adam, though. They said it two years prior when my elder sister, Corvetta, had been a part of the morning news team. She tried to be an effective news anchor but also advocated for the diverse set of talents that the team held. She wanted to record a video of herself singing. There was a private discussion between her and the instructors, and instead she recorded little personal tapes on the school property that she kept in a little shoebox by her bed: I found it while snooping. She didn't return to the morning news team the next semester. People might suggest it is because my sister struggled with her self-esteem at the time, or that she wasn't the best in the class, or that she tended to skip school and cut class as often as possible to run around with her friends from the block. But the hurt she held when she said that an instructor felt that she didn't talk "proper" enough for the camera was real. By the time Adam joined the team, maybe he was just a bit more pushy, or maybe he had more evidence that this sort of thing would work if we put attention behind their students, or maybe it was because he *was* a student athlete for the baseball team. Whatever it was, he made things happen. Things didn't happen to him.

The student body reacted differently from the faculty expressions. We all had a favorite Adam Little skit. It was like having our own

YouTuber in the halls. He became a micro-celebrity. The skits reached our rivals and neighbors at Briggs. Adam could be spotted at games with a camera, a tripod, an aluminized screen, and a single mic that held a golden rule: never let it go, hold on to it like it is your lifeline.

When Adam Little left the morning news, citing creative differences, we speculated what might've happened. It might have been because he took the aim of the channel away from the intention: teaching students about journalism and broadcasting. I suspect it had something to do with how targeted his skits eventually became. Writers write what they know is the parable. He wrote who he knew. A skit landed on the morning news that snuck past the censors: it was a smear job at a girl, an ex-girlfriend, who'd been allegedly following him. The skit starred Adam Little and MarShawn McCarrel, and the girl was left humiliated once it became extremely obvious who it was about within the student body. It only took a couple of tweets before people were called into the office to answer some questions—it's also how we figured out that the faculty were making false profiles to monitor the students on social media.

It didn't matter that Adam Little left, though; he already had a substantial reputation as a funny guy. But it piqued my interests. I signed up for the morning news team on the grounds of my sister's participation and my reputation in the Accelerated English program. I was admitted along with three of my other classmates. We joined several other athletes within the program who were taking the class for credits.

Our first assignment was memorizing the process for getting content on the air. Our central duo were our anchors, who never had to record anything they didn't want to. Their job was to report the information the administration needed to get to the student body. They would become the most familiar faces for the student body for a month. Then we had our forecasters, who checked the temperature and reported incoming weather reports for the school. Then we had reporters who created something for the content calendar every two weeks. We could report on anything, but we had to report on something: games, band practice, concerns of the student body.

And then we had the script.

Scripting was the most loathed position among the team. It was largely about rendering something useful for the morning anchors. You checked the emails for press releases from the faculty and club leaders, you rendered them into something useful, you kept abreast of the timing for the anchors. You removed names and added names in accordance with who was present and who was tardy or absent in the team. You were not the voice of the room; you were its mind.

It was being a writer, plain and simple.

It was something I hadn't noticed I developed a skill for. I just thought everyone else moved slower. But many people fumbled at the script phase and my teachers found themselves asking me to look over whatever was drafted and do quick edits or give structural feedback before we went live. It never felt like a chore, and I also never felt like I ought to be charging people for this kind of thing. It just felt like something other people didn't want to do and I did. I always knocked this out in the first twenty minutes of class, also so I could focus on my own weekly segment that I'd developed or figuring out what content could set me up to match the prestige of Adam Little.

See, once Adam Little left, we started receiving hate comments on many of our portals. A lot of students wanted the morning news to be funny again. The morning news took up maybe fifteen to twenty minutes of the second-period coursework and while some teachers loved the brief hiatus to do more prep, others felt it detracted from quality learning and would turn it off if students were uninterested. We had an attention economy. I fielded the complaints from both sides of our faculty, the Black students who felt like I was besmirching Adam's legacy, and the students in my Honors level who felt like our work was distracting by promoting the lowest common denominators of our community: the prominently Black athletes on the graduation track.

"You don't get it because you're one of the *popular kids*," they said. It was the first time anyone ever described me as such, and it certainly was the only time. It rubbed me wrong in a way I couldn't place at the time. A way to demean me for the choices and perceptions of other people rather than anything I said or believed. To say something without saying it, an infliction that feels particularly jaded as "Boy" and "Blacks" with an S.

One student among this collective who ought to have known better made it his entire ambition to mock the systems that the Black majority of the student athletics leaned into. When Whitney Houston died in 2012, he denigrated my decisions as an anchor for the morning news and the head of my original segment, "World Issues with Steven Underwood," to highlight the death and contributions of this woman without smearing her for a drug overdose.

"She was a crackhead," he said in a private conversation. It was the start and finish of his argument. It was my first run-in with the concept of how a word could not be a slur of race but still manifest the inhumanity of one. The kind of word, a slogan, a slang, that collected the choices of one person and mixed them with societal failures that create the choices just to beat them with them altogether. It made no room for empathy or humanity. When I retorted the importance of a figure to Black identity and music, how the contributions of an important figure cannot or should not be surmised by how their personal choices impacted them, rather than groups of people who must contend with the harm that those choices made, he sneered again.

"Okay, but she was a crackhead. Does being a Black crackhead matter more than being a crackhead?" I walked away from the conversation to do the highlight anyway. Most of the student body thanked me for it throughout the day. From then on at the school, people who knew me only as "Alexis's younger brother" knew me as just "Steven."

By the end of the year, others called me the last good thing about the morning news segment.

That kid hopped onto Twitter to further his denigration. "I can't believe people are boo-hooing just because one more crackhead overdosed. Duh, that's what happens when you do drugs."

A friend of ours with more than one thousand followers—a lot for that time and for our school—retweeted it, but twote: "My #LRT is a dickhead." His followers joined in, calling him a number of rude names. There was some commotion that followed—an argument and an accusation of cyberbullying—but the tweets have since been deleted and none of us were nosey enough to follow up with what happened.

Sometime later, when I tied with our would-be valedictorian Brandi in the student body president elections for the Class of 2023 (to the cheers of my mother), that same kid remarked that it was because I was Black. Not even popular. "Our own Barack Obama," he said, smiling. It's one of the moments I noticed how far apart the distance of his teeth were.

I called him racist. He said he couldn't be racist, because he was Jewish, and everyone knew Jews were slaves for longer than Black people were. "You all think you own being slaves."

This time, he didn't tweet it. He kept this comment between us under flickering fluorescent lights, where most racism thrives like mold.

Another of our classmates, a white boy who was "down," told me that he didn't vote for me because I was Black. "It was because I fucking hate Brandi. I'd rather you win than her and I don't even like you. I actually hate you, Steven."

He wasn't just an athlete. He was also an AP kid—a particular talent with math and the hard sciences, where I was peppered for the humanities and life sciences.

Me and this boy were not friends until we were adults, and he confessed (while crossfaded at a housewarming) that his hatred of me was largely from a feeling that he didn't belong among our group of Black friends. He felt I got to come by proxy of being Black when he wasn't, and, thus, he had to show everyone I didn't belong. He failed.

A few months later, one of our advisors sat me down to see if I would abdicate my seat as copresident of the student council. "Brandi just needs it more than you for her personal record. You understand, right? She has big dreams when it comes to college."

I didn't. I wondered about my own dreams. What I would do after high school, who would stick up for me in this room about how unfair it was to ask—to pressure—a teenager to commit to the greater good of some white girl who was never *particularly* nice to me, who had the GPA and the extracurriculars and potentially the support to apply to Ivy League schools. How my opportunities were limited to the places I could get to by foot—from library volunteering to election day booth working to community tutoring initiatives and learning to code websites over the summer while working at McDonalds.

I wasn't allowed to leave the room until I said yes. No one said I couldn't leave. They just kept smiling, nodding, and reminding me of the innate goodness I have always exhibited. By the end of the hour-and-a-half-long meeting, I was treasurer of the student council, and Brandi was the president. I felt most Black walking home from school to shatter the joy of my mother.

They'd already made a habit of seeing the ways I was not as Black as they expected: from their selective choice channel of BET to our classmates. They also expected, on some level, that my disinterest in athletics also alienated me further from my Blackness. In their minds, they dressed me as an Urkel and a Stefan, never a Steven. They saw me cowering at the idea of poverty and the hood, in their heads, and on the trade up to their whiteness. They reached down beneath my belt to take something they coveted, that they thought I knew nothing of the worth. What they didn't know was that there were costs to even touching this thing, to hold on their hands the fortunes of men and women whose backs couldn't shiver under the pressure they folded under. A lineage of analysts and strategists, thieves and killers, who turned as sweet as cunning when the world was sour. They didn't know that the hoods I walked with impunity had more to them than what they saw as the grotesque disparity between the intellectual and the barbaric. What they were seeing was the choices Black people made early that weren't the choice at all: to game a system that saw itself as flawless or to resist it at the suffering of everyone beneath it.

It made utter sense why I got out of the way. All the spotlight in the world couldn't save me from the reality that in the most important situations, I can say yes, but I am powerless.

/////////

On March 5, 2012, a production company called Invisible Children dropped *Kony 2012*. It was a campaign to capture or kill Ugandan warlord Joseph Kony. It was intense in its pathos, snatching tears from the open teen spirit of the time. Some might say it was orchestrated to go viral. Because it was.

"Nothing is more powerful than an idea whose time has come. Nothing is more powerful than an idea whose time is now."

Open on a global spiraling on a backdrop as black as pitch with an illumination behind the sphere and a globe so dark, lit at the social epicenters of the planet. A man's voice breaks the melodic music: "Right now, there are more people on Facebook than there were on the planet two hundred years ago. Humanity's greatest desire is to belong and to connect. And now we see each other. We hear each other. We share what we love, and it reminds us what we have in common."[2]

Following this, we see clips on YouTube. A four-year-old kid rescued in Haiti. A toddler rallying self-faith: even you will know how to ride a bike. A twenty-nine-year-old deaf woman weeping at the sound of her voice. The united message is the joy of connection.

Then, a countdown: white font, black backdrop. A call to try something new, to empower a new way of doing things that terrifies the old guys in suits.

In the next twenty-seven minutes, we were going to learn how to use a platform to stop an African dictator and change the world. A popular freshman girl named Brittany spearheaded this issue at our school. She raised money to order a kit, and she maintained a puncturing focus on the ongoing news from Invisible Children for the coming date of activation. I was raised Jehovah's Witness, and the mobilization reminded me of the coming Judgment Day.

The hope was equally as sanctimonious. There would come a day when mass protest will take place. We teenagers would storm the streets, raise our voices, and demand the United Nations do something about Joseph Kony. We would march, scream, and borrow the great radicalism of the Civil Rights Movement until blood dried on Joseph Kony's wrath.

One month prior, just twenty-one days after his seventeenth birthday, Trayvon Martin went to visit his father and his soon-to-be stepmother's townhouse in Sanford, Florida. Trayvon Martin was a Dade County kid, a predominantly Black community that has turned out future Black creatives like Kid Fury of *The Read* and Barry Jenkins and Tarell Alvin McCraney of the Oscar-winning film *Moonlight.*

There are many things Trayvon's family has come to say about him. That he was a hero who pulled his father out of a burning apartment. That he was an avid gamer. That he washed cars and babysat and played football. That he was an All-American boy save for the then out-of-the-ordinary characteristic of being Black. His coaches called him shy, always in a hoodie and easily enchanted by music. That Trayvon Martin was a gifted engineer, whose mechanical gifts assembled and disassembled bikes around the neighborhood. The village said that Martin enrolled in the seven-week program in Opa-Locka, Florida, called "Experience Aviation." Opa-Locka, being an aviation hub founded under the innovations and dreams of aviation experts, became the perfect place to refine these visions and gifts. His dreams of aerospace pulled him away from the typical tools of success with football to refine the mind it'd take to bring the gift of flight to the world. He transferred schools to bring this vision to life. Martin's own teachers came forward to dispel the illusions that would surface around him. He was a normal kid. A well-behaved kid. A kid who passed his classes. But these illusions are ill equipped to frame the unfairness of his circumstances.

Martin was a teenage boy. Sometimes, you get into shit while trying to figure out the balance between what you want to do and what you should do. He'd been suspended for having a pipe on him with an empty baggy of weed—just weed. Most white kids in my high school had worse in their backpacks—a sandwich baggy of Percocet and another baggy halfway to the brim with shrooms.

Martin had been suspended for tardiness, truancy, and jotting "W.T.F." on a door. Nothing big. I'd seen people do worse. Once, Martin had been found with a backpack of jewelry and a screwdriver that a school snitch—what folk would call a "school officer"—called a burglary tool. When asked, he said a friend gave it to him and didn't say anything else. No one came to collect anything. No reports followed up. Nothing.

A reporter, Deborah Acosta of the *Miami Herald*, published an article called "What Trayvon Martin's Tweets Say About Him," which detailed thousands of tweets where Martin—called Slimm on this account—existed. Largely, this was in response to conservative websites like *The Daily Caller* leaking these details in a smear campaign. He was vulgar and edgy and loved Black comedies—namely, the *Friday* franchise. He wholly said fuck Krop Senior High. And he clearly designed himself a pretty boy, keen on love and keener on sex without any real experience of what these things meant. Overall, he was a typical childish teen with a sweet tooth.

Of all of the unfortunate things mentioned, very little attention was paid to his sweet tooth, despite how much it mattered to where he was, who he was and the why, in the end, he was.

Grievingly, what came after these posts gave reason for the back-and-forth of hyperbole: the cutting and calculation of a young man's expectantly complicated humanity.

On February 26, 2012, Trayvon Martin was gunned down by George Zimmerman and the #BlackLivesMatter movement was born.

Before Trayvon died, he'd purchased sweets: a bag of Skittles (45g total sugar) and a watermelon Arizona Iced Tea (20g total sugar).

We learned so much about Trayvon Martin's life, but we did not learn about his fear. My mother's first fiancé told me about the panic of being shot. He was quite clear, a solemn and gentle man with a passion for images in his words. He talked about the biting of the flesh when something hot runs through the nerves and singes them till they go cold. He put three rough fingers on my collarbone and pressed until pain became numb. He held my brown eyes in his own, cornrows nappy and greased under the kitchen lamp. With broad lips, he said:

> Hot in your body like a kettle. You want to pull it out and when you can't you get real scared. And you try to think about how brave it look on TV. But when you think you're dying, you know what real is like. Death don't care about how much of a man you are or what your skin is. It just cares what you feel. You feel afraid. And either you live or die. And the world decides if you a man or not after.

The world didn't call Trayvon a man. It called him a monster. A lot of people felt different after that.

What is the measure of a human's existence and the wrongs or rights that they've inflicted and cherished in only seventeen years of existence when his sole crime was to be Black in the shadow of night became the talking point of an entire country. With every headline and every question and every debate and every post, I became aware of something no request for abdication or claim of a post-racial society could disperse: a radical notion that I'd been caught asleep in a bed of nightmares.

"Slacktvism" became the word to define what the SJWs were getting into. The idea that activism is not real if it isn't offline and solely exists in the context of self-righteous grandstanding, like what followed the release of *Kony 2012*. Slacktivism is about stunts rather than actions. It is loud and draws attention but never attracts actual change. And all of the people present can be having fun, but it doesn't mean a thing. And that's what's dangerous about the concept if we are all discussing something enjoyable: Are we discussing the hard work of impacting change through the limited hands we have ready at the scene?

For a while in 2012, Kony became a vindication that Black Lives Matter—the concept surrounding Trayvon Martin's death rather than the hashtag or movement, that energy of what to make of losing Black life while Obama was president—could only be a temporary farce, a single blip in a wider see of riveting echoes.

By the end of 2012, it was slacktivism that was put to rest and in the next two years, social media would be the grounds of the most prominent push for social activism.

WE ARE FINNA GO GET LIT, SIS

Memes are perhaps the most important currency to the internet. It is also the lifeblood of what it means to be a part of an online community. Black culture and Black art are no different, and, as with many of our issues, it is never without its own controversies. Namely, we face the controversy of cosplay with Blackness in a world where your Blackness can merely be a suggestion.

In 2015, blackface was the nature of that woman, Rachel Dolezal, obtaining positions by centering herself as transracial during a period where the public disagreed on the increasing mainstream visibility of trans identity. Involuntarily, she became a meme. In response, there were people who believed that the world was full of actual Black people deeply invested in divesting from Blackness. They named folks like Stacey Dash, Candace Owens, and their ilk of Black conservatives. Others made jokes about transracialism, pointing out the hypocrisy of how such a conditional existence can only mirror caricature. However, more stories came to light about the number of Black women in academic positions who suffered from the deception that is and was Rachel Dolezal. She took roles from them. She took space from them. She took leadership from them. And those were only her crimes pretending to be a Black woman.

In 2002, Dolezal sued Howard University for discrimination based on race. She believed she was denied scholarships and other positions of power because she was a part of an unfavorable class: she was a white woman.

When the world revealed the obvious—Rachel was never Black—there were many Black women who pointed out the harassment and pain she subjected them to. Rachel Dolezal couldn't stand to cosplay a kind Black woman. In most respects, she seemed to be an "angry" one. Empowered by the trope, even. After she was exposed, she snatched more opportunity, more focus, more energy from Black women than necessary. In these opportunities, she trafficked and communicated the tokens of Black womanhood: bamboo earrings, locs down her back, the slang and aesthetic of Black femininity. But, as she did so, she did not build upon the honesty of a person. Carefully and particularly, she built her social capital with the tokens of Black womanhood. She spent those tokens lavishly. And never in the breath of her existence did she have to care about Black issues, especially once the truth of her birth as a white woman came out. She could talk like one of us, she could act like one of us, and she might say, "Black lives matter," here and there, but no one had to make room for the space that Blackness takes.

Rachel Dolezal could be a kind of Black woman that required zero capital in Blackness. She only went viral for a relatively small amount of time and in that time, Dolezal introduced blackface to the digital arts era.

During an interview on *TMZ*, Antoine Dodson commented that he didn't agree with the concept of digital blackface, or discouraging white people from using Black memes to mock Blackness in tone, if not outright in identity.

Writer Aisha Harris discussed the allure of blackface, particularly in memes, during an interview with Jason Parham. She suggested this phenomenon revolved around a "persistent, if unconscious, desire to see Black people perform."

In the discussion, Antoine Dodson centered his experiences profiting in appearances and hosting opportunities for his meme.

> If it wasn't for white people in the first place, I wouldn't have been as big as I was and still is. And they pay a lot of money also if they consider [you] [a] meme, like I can say that when I'm hired to go on different gigs: white people typically pay top dollar and I'm super comfortable. . . . As for my own skin people, it's a joke to them. I rarely go to Black events, let's clearly be honest. . . . If white people wanted to make a joke about me, they could have. But when I go on these events in these different places to host: I don't get that they're making fun of me. First of all, I'm not finna put you in a first class hotel: if I'm making a joke out of you.[3]

Dodson seems confused in this interview. Perhaps it is an issue of the one who asked him the question. Perhaps it is a sign of Dodson's own history with digital blackface—his comments do not really disagree with someone who has made almost a decade-long career as a meme. Someone who rejects proximity to Black culture and Black people, while centering money and profit as the only reason to exist. My mother once said that people who stand for nothing will fall for anything. There's a kind of truth to this lesson as an artist. You must know the difference between hope and humor, which is to say you have to be able to tell when you are the butt of a joke, and when you are the center of attention. One might say this includes knowing when the price point involved is solely to be a joke for a room full of people, but that isn't for just anyone to conclude. And it isn't all the way the point.

Digital blackface has very little to do with the mockery that white people make of Blackness. It has something, though.

When writers like Aisha Harris and Lauren Michele Jackson discuss digital blackface, they discuss mostly the act of credit. For the most part, they respect the transportation of language and culture and how identity functions when in close proximity—especially with how much social media relies on Blackness to exist as an intriguing statement. They look at how the Blackness of the character they are emulating is discarded along with the negative parts of that existence. Everyone wants to be Black, until it is time to be Black.

I watched the *Halloweentown* film series as a child. I liked *Halloweentown 2: Kalabar's Revenge* most. The story revolves around monsters who cursed humans who would dress up as them for Halloween to mock them. There's something cryptically mythic about this story—as Arachne was punished for humiliating the gods. You read the story and think Athena is a vain monster for what she did, ignoring how it might be for a god to have their humanity dwarfed by those their existence has been chained to. The men in masks had to be punished because the men in masks had no idea who or what they were hurting.

It was an enchanting suggestion, a mile in the shoes of the oppressed. A changeling narrative. One would think the nature of this would enchant online. However, this is the horror of this act. Change your avi to a Black woman. Use our GIFs and reaction memes. Talk like us, act like us. The web of anti-Blackness will never truly touch you, because the act of anti-Blackness harms those who see the deep spiritual fiber of Blackness as a necessity. An existence you stand on with every fiber of your pulsating life. It is why, online, Blackness cannot *not* exist. It is why the Black kids sit together in the cafeteria and thus converge on any platform.

This is a stroll not just anyone can do. You've got to be incorporated. And where you are incorporated, you see where the shield rusts, suffers, and shatters.

It is ironic that digital blackface is a phenomenon that mostly impacts Black women, but an outlet like *TMZ* reached into the dregs of the internet to discuss the concept with Dodson, rather than someone like former Viner Peaches Monroee (real name Kayla Newman), who coined the term "eyebrows on fleek."[4] Her story is one of the sporadic opportunities on the internet. On June 20, 2014, she'd just returned from the nail salon with her mother where she received an eyebrow threading and wax. She was feeling herself, and so she opened her phone and recorded a selfie video for the app.

"We in this bitch, finna get crunk. Eyebrows on fleek. The fuck?"

Six seconds. Nothing was on her mind. She just wanted to stunt for a second, feel beautiful, celebrate, and memorialize for no one other than herself. It went viral from there. And for the first month, some people didn't know what "on fleek" meant. They called it "ratchet" when ratchetness was mocked. Some Black men put on thick lipstick and wigs and re-created the sound. But, eventually, the hate of irony bred into authenticity. Those men made careers wearing wigs and dresses, and Peaches was eventually free to have fun. There is no bad ending to a story like that.

March 1, 2015, Nicki Minaj took to Instagram to playfully call out Christina Milian for selling T-shirts that said "Pretty on Fleek" and not cutting the Barb a check for her "Feeling Myself" feature where she said "Pretty on fleek"—simultaneously not using the phrase correctly while also cementing its popularity as a zeitgeist rather than just another meme. They had a tongue-in-cheek back-and-forth. However, everyone pointed out a consistent fact: this meme belonged to neither one of them. No one thought either of them erased Peaches on purpose, but it still happened. White creators often had the benefit of the behind-the-scenes support of agents, management, and curators. But Black creators rarely had the same treatment. In the early days of the YouTube subculture, when the Partner Program rolled out, whatever profits these amateur artists snatched were aided by the vision of others. Black creators had to figure it out on their own. This involved more than just being funny: this involved business filings, copyright paperwork, media pushes. Did you know just to launch a merch line, you'd need to file an LLC and take the time to curate a manufacturer and enough start-up capital to fund a bulk purchase *and* the storage space to house the merchandise?

On Twitter, users demanded that people properly credit Peaches Monroee for her intellectual property. That thought they were helping. This battle encompassed something noted before Vine burned down as a business and a culture. With only six seconds of attention, most of what they did was attested to the art of memes: the art of a moment. When a potato flies around a room, if someone did not spend six seconds observing it, did it exist at all? Is it worth anything on a Twitter or a YouTube? Could it make money, and, if it does, who deserves to be paid?

Peaches, who was very much to herself, resolved to keep to herself. She couldn't truly ever make enough noise for anyone to care. When a brand made sure to properly credit a person for their work, they made sure to be liable to pay them for their work. They made sure to acknowledge who and what made such an art capable of being done. And it isn't to say that businesses at the time didn't invest in creators. They did. However, who they invested in also came with stipulations, expectations, and inferences. Black audiences rarely rewarded silence on Black issues. Black audiences came with things that could potentially confuse someone not in the know. With Black audiences comes a loyalty that could be fickle . . . if you forget to care that people are on the other end.

And that's why Twitter, though it'd help against someone like Nicki Minaj, a Black woman who ought to have known better, or done better, or showed support, acts as one of the better mediums for call-out culture: to question the ability of the powerful to do something, and to show them how the question could easily become action.

While two celebrity musicians debated the theft of a creator's property online, Peaches simply watched and waited. Her IP would be infringed again by companies like Forever 21, in T-shirts and other fast-fashion merchandise.

In 2018, Peaches Monroee launched a GoFundMe for a cosmetic and haircare line. In the description, she made an impassioned call:

> Everyone has used the phrase/word but I haven't received any money behind it or recognition. So it brings me to say that I want to start a cosmetic and hair extension line; But I don't have any money to do so. Just so everyone can know my plans, with this money I plan on starting a website, get this project on legal papers with a good team of lawyers, etc and making sure my dreams come true as far as this "Fleek" thing. I feel like this is my second chance and I will not mess this up. I know this is going to take hard work and dedication. But I do want to sell beautiful products to the beautiful people in this world.[5]

She received backlash. Some thought she was being greedy by demanding money for a meme. Most people pointed out that a donation is not the same as a demand, and that intellectual property is still property. In the end, she raised upward of $16,880. More than what she made before, not nearly her worth.

Following Peaches's graceful exit from the spotlight, the internet decided to keep the aesthetic. Peaches spoke to BET about the impact of her meme: "You can search and see. You can search 'fleek' and I pop up. It throws me a little curveball, but I also [try] to see it as free advertisement. Since I went viral, I started my own business at a young age. I wanted to make sure I have the right hair, the right website. I wanted to make sure that everything on fleek."[6]

Her impact on the cosmetics industry is plain. More hair and eyebrow lines exist under the nomenclature of "fleek" than any other passing trend. She is the voice of Black self-love in the digital age while also being aware of the pitfalls that occur when ownership is not given properly to who made an idea. Between celebrities fighting over ownership of an idea and big brands shelling out merchandise, there is a minimum of a million dollars that have been deprived along with brand deals and endorsements that grease the engines of the digital marketplace. In 2023, Taraji P. Henson highlighted how much more Tyler Perry paid her, more than she'd ever been paid before in her life, as an Oscar award–winning A-list celebrity. However, it is just as quickly pointed out that she was still not paid her worth.

Almost certainly there is a difference.

This begets an idea that what Black creatives—especially Black women—face in the limelight is an oppression of time and capability. In a capitalist society, to neglect the worth of an individual is to reinforce a hierarchy of power. It is to say no one sees much contribution to that person—or that group. In entertainment, Black artists face this concept as the "Black tax" or the idea that being Black makes your creation and labor less valuable. You will not likely receive your fair share of reward in equity or respect for the work you do. It is a concept that is as much as a stock of entertainment and art as the concept of the white gaze, as manifested by the author Toni Morrison.

It doesn't mean that individuals are not as successful as their brands might seem as suggested by people who say that those who are not paid their worth or commissioned are complaining over what their actual backgrounds cannot sustain. It is to say that people with access to money or respect for the Black people who construct these ideas, trends, and movements deny these things as a theft of Black existence. By any name, it is widely considered aesthetic slavery at worst and an apartheid at best. These issues during an era where social media became the grounds for discussion and dissection of racialized atrocities by the state and popular culture, where wokeness had become so co-opted as a marketing scam that the presumption of neutrality in most cases was tantamount to actual offense, significantly contributed to the notion that disagreements with digital blackface was less about mocking Blackness and more about the numerous real Black people punished for being ourselves where whiteness in cosplay is rewarded with personality and profits.

Enter influencers like former Viner Landon Romano, who became popular through a string of caricatures divorced of authenticity while embodying a particular stock trope: the ratchet Black girl. Landon is easily meme-able, even when what he cultivates does not hold the art or the value that those who came before him in a more authentic light did. This authenticity has nothing to do with how he speaks, or what he governs his speech—rather, what topics and what niches he has ownership of. While he might borrow heavily from the AAVE of his classmates and friends, he has never upheld any semblance of the misogynoir by proxy of kin or bodily trauma. A lamb does not sharpen its horns and run with rhinos. However, what was offered in Landon—and all influencers of his kind—was an opportunity for an audience to participate in the colorful cosplay of Black womanhood without the guilt of the imagery. What he offered to brands was a parody of the people that they would be selling to without the trouble of depicting troubling notions. And Landon leaned into this, never admitting just how his caricature impacted the Black women he replaced, or how he did not offer a challenge to corporations who asked in the first place for the satire of Blackness to ever be centered without confronting the truth of who contributes to the circumstances.

A ratchet image cannot exist in a world where wealth is equally distributed and power flows as freely to women as it might to men.

Landon's character has props: tight pants, sloppy makeup, bandannas crudely tied around the hairline. He exaggerates his speech. He offers sass. He does the neckroll and twerks a whole lot of nothing uncoordinatedly. Granted, Landon has never once darkened his skin. He has never once clarified that the character he was portraying was a Black woman. However, with caricature, the act of explaining what you are describing defeats the purpose of the alleged satire. If you tuck your shirt through the neckline, let limp your wrist, and pop your tongue, do you need to say you are portraying a gay man, or does the performance lead the way to a narrative of beliefs?

Romano was born in Baton Rouge, Louisiana. There is no mistaking that, by chance, he might've come across plenty of authentic lives of Black women. In fact, Landon Romano is vocal that this is how he came across in his manner and speaking.

> My accent and my attitude is just who I am. I'm from Louisiana, went to high school in Mississippi. Shit is different down there. This is just how I was raised. Sometimes ppl get offended & think that just bc I'm a white male im supposed to act a certain kind of way. I understand that not all white ppl where y'all are from act like i do. But y'all have to understand my upbringing. ME & the bitch from Bella Noche are from the same city lol. Everybody is influenced by their surroundings during their upbringing. I just so happened to be brought up around a lot of black folks. We all got along and cut up together in Louisiana. I'm sure plenty of my lingo came from them and I would never discredit them on that.[7]

A Black person responded: "Omfg you even said black 'Folks' just like my grandma. A true southerner." Another said: "U aint got to explain yourself to MFs."

Perhaps that's how he came across the Blaccent like a Mississippi Iggy Azalea. Perhaps that's where he entertained the persona of a Southern stripper. One user on a video calling out Romano's hood-ratchet embodiment commented that Landon is from the South with a bubbly and flamboyant personality. That he wears Fashion Nova because he likes it, that he is a drag queen maybe or that he isn't prissy and ladylike and that doesn't mean he is channeling Black caricature.

In the same video, dressed in yellow army fatigues, he chants, "PERIOD!" at the top of his lungs in the middle of a Sherman Oaks neighborhood for 25.7k retweets and 49.5k likes. His entire outfit came from PrettyLittleThing, as he clarified in the comments. His Twitter account at the time was a wall of rehearsal, a portrait of method acting as he refined the points of this character. For example: on September 8, 2014, Landon Romano twote to the world the extremely relevant and authentic observation: "YOUR BITCH JUST GOT PAID AYYYYYEEE FINNA GET THIS HAIR DID."[8]

His posts aren't all in Black voice. When he is addressing the contributions of the Black community on his channels, his diction is adequately respectful and foreign:

"Black people invented the music industry. And that's just facts."[9]

When Joe Biden won the 2020 presidential election, Landon Romano twote: "Black people won this race for us period"[10] and "A black women just got elected as Vice President. History has just been made. I'm crying."[11]

May 27, 2020, Landon Romano showed his support for the George Floyd protests. "I don't give a fuck who looting out of target or whatever the fuck. there is a bigger picture here black people are being murdered !!!! #ICantBreathe."[12]

In 2018, Landon Romano addressed the accusations sporadically, because of course not everyone was blinded by the very thin veil. "NOT ALL BLACK WOMEN ACT ALIKE. NOT ALL WHITE WOMEN ACT LIKE. NOT ALL WHITE MEN ACT LIKE. NOT ALL BLACK MEN ACT ALIKE. Stop grouping everybody into one mf category. We were all raised differently, in different environments, & different circumstances. What the fuck yall don't get."[13]

Later, Romano would continue his endorsement of the Black creators with a vocal statement that did not go as viral as his usual performance art. "As grateful as I am for the overwhelming amount of brand deal offers I have received in the last few months, I can't help but wonder if black influencers get the same amount of love from these brands. I really hope so. It just got me thinking."

"I do not accept all of the offers obviously. And I have referred several brands to other influencers who are black. But if you have any talented black influencers who you think are not getting the paper they deserve let me know so I can note that for future."[14]

In the past, Romano received a Chili's endorsement. He collaborated with fashion brands and cosmetic surgeons for fillers, veneers, and lip injections. Softly, as his brand became more refined, he made more videos in his "natural" voice. He got approved for a web series with the Black-owned gossip blog *The Shade Room*, where he would serve as a Judge-Judy-esque character in one of his established ratchet caricatures. He filmed one episode (as of 2025), and the show is slated as "in-development" still. He left Los Angeles once his pivot to mainstream did not go as well and wound up in Nashville. He dropped a song that did lukewarm at most. He debuted his Black best friend—as customary. He is followed by several celebrities—Jhene Aiko, Kylie Jenner, and more. And, most importantly, remained silent regarding issues on Blackness and protest. In a vide, where Romano plays a love-spurned babymother weeping over an unfaithful or undesiring man, Romano cradles a brown-skinned baby and screams about pregnancy before manhandling the toddler like a football. A stock character of the Welfare Queen with 79,859 likes.

Before I think about Landon Romano, I think about the business of branding behind memeing that Antoine Dodson discussed. He drew a line in the sand where cancel culture would impact his business and claimed race did not matter, while highlighting the racial demographic of who paid him for his performance. I think about the doors that Rachel Dolezal walked through when she dressed herself in the image of a Black woman, and all of its spirituality. Then, I think about Landon Romano and what he's gained. I think about the opportunities denied to Black women who are authentically themselves. I think about how cheap the art becomes when the final word doesn't come from the creators' lips. I think about what is for sale when the merchant has no understanding of what is on their shelves. When the merchant knows only that people will pay for the idea of something, without the people.

I think that's the point in the end. In this country, at least, you can create a culture by erasing another one laugh at a time.

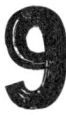

Do that little dance your Titi loves.

—A BLACK MATRON

LIKE EVERYONE'S WATCHING

Black folk love to move. We love to sense.

It's in our bones, some shivering vibrations as native as our heart-beat. It's a laugh from your forehead to your toes. Something that sure must be right because you sure have to do it.

Dancing is as native to me as breathing. So natural I mistrust all institutions that tell me to sit still. For years, little Black kids steal moments of rebellion in the schoolhouses to make their own mistrust known. In the hallways, at sixteen, girls kick up one leg and hook the air like a nine iron stroking sharp white globes across green turf.

They chant. "Aye!" They burst. "Aye!" Two heels into the earth, they do a little jig. Our grandmothers did it in their day. My grandma Kandi Kane tells me how ain't nothing new under the sun. They don't fixate on anything sexual in the act, like they know the innocuous shape of their bodies elicits sexuality on the streets. Like the grown men in Philly who kept telling my sisters they got some hips over the summer and my aunties sighed to them—

Welcome to the real world.

Black boys snatch a beat with those same beaten bones that could one day crack on night sticks and concrete and matched the brittle wood clenching black lead. They made a beat, a rattling staccato off the cuff. They know that wood smacks louder than plastic like they know a nightclub stings differently than a tabletop.

Drummer Boys and Dancer Girls.

Beat Boys and Chanting Girls.

For Black folk, dance is aggressive and gender fluid. In high school, my friend Jamil was the best twerker in the class. Not just in the way Black teen boys know. Black folk know catching a twerk is not an immobile act. It is not a lap dance, though it can seem like it is to someone intent on criminalizing all passion. You have to follow. It's a dance where you have to be intent on paying attention to your partner. You have maybe seven seconds to find their rhythm and join in. More often than not, it's too much to handle. And the dance becomes communal. Your friends—hopefully your best friend—catches you, supports you, uplifts you. And the fullness of two people's weight is given a chariot of the community until the song ends. And it's your turn to do the same at least once before the night ends. Together, your friends collect imaginary dance cards and talk—who got the most dances, which is to say, who had enough courage to get their asses off the wall and ask a girl if she wanted to dance. You'll get more Nos than you'll get yeses and you hope to be humble about your Ls.

Tall and lithe, with braces fielding his teeth and cold brown skin, Jamil always had a joke. Between third and fourth period, he'd throw it back on the locker doors and never face the scrutiny of his masculinity. Because he was a baller. And who was gonna beat his ass?

Let there have been a camera on him. Let there have been a Tik-Tok or a Vine. Jamil'd have hopped on that damn tabletop and got loose. He'd have been Dario Boatner, or ObeyDario on Vine—hitting it for 'em one time in a high school hallway one era and in the next dancing in Volumes 3 and 4 of *Savage X Fenty* by Rihanna, with The Weeknd for Super Bowl LV, again with Rihanna for Super Bowl LVII, and some award shows such as the Billboard Music Awards. You don't immediately notice it's him when he dances. Something about his smile is quite familiar, about the bravado he has in his isolations, but in the end, he is another short light-skinned kid in a sea of others. One of the many Black dancers in LA classically trained to be in the background and only appear as talented as the star in the spotlight.

One time, while running around with the camera from our morning news broadcast—"FHHS News," for whom I was a student reporter and thus iconically recognizable across the campus—I'd recorded him and my friends during first period dancing for YouTube. It was a small dance video, a trailer. I thought about how viral it'll go and how we should do something a lot more interesting with access to a camera and editing software through the school. That video is a memorial of our boyhood friendship—that type of thing between Black boys who want to be men. These bodies committed to electricity have weathered storms; we've hit the deck in high grass fields to dodge the cops when we were running the streets pass curfew; we'd been stalked through showrooms and malls by security; we'd been told by white girls we barely even glanced at for directions around their school that they'd never date Black guys as they giggled and ran the other direction from us. We never made another video. I see them when I go home on holidays.

Dance is the freest instrument of Blackness ever known.

We have been detained by our teachers for this freedom. Beaten by our mothers and our grandmothers for it. On an episode of *Atlanta*, Donald Glover pens a Black boy chastised by his mama for dancing on the tables in school. He writes the Sapphire Mother as if to say: These white people will kill you.

In 2013, Miley Cyrus starts twerking for her musical comeback and escape from the squeaky, unserious Disney glimmer from her era as Hannah Montana, the blonde, brightly dressed fictional pop-rock star for television. An era that was once impossible for Disney stars to hold, as Hilary Duff says, because Disney did not want its stars doing multiple things like music. But with stars like Hilary Duff and Raven Symone pulling out all the stops, she was almost designed to be a music star.

Cyrus's music video for "We Can't Stop" showcases a party heavy with drugs and alcohol and twerking Black women—the hallmarks of a bad girl era for white people. Black folks point out how close the lyrics sound to "Can't Stop, Won't Stop" from Bad Boy. Her father congratulates Miley Cyrus for inventing twerking and says he would've done it, too, in her day in that same country twang he says everything; Black folks point out how she never invented anything. In fact, Miley hasn't done it close to correctly. She's too stiff. Perhaps with practice, she'll loosen up a bit more. Still, *Glee* does an episode, acknowledging Miley as an expert twerker. Miley Cyrus escapes her Hannah Montana era. People attribute Miley Cyrus as popularizing something she's never done correctly. That she didn't even have the care to turn into community. Perhaps it's not her fault, but a director's. I don't know her director and celebrity is about making a person into an enterprise and referring to teams by the name of who they serve. And, so, I blame Miley Cyrus twerking on the VMA stage in 2013 and I held it against her for so long that I almost missed her iconic album *Plastic Hearts* until I heard "Midnight Sky" twinkling bass into a gritty pop-rock ballad while taking a lover early 2022 in a blacked-out Columbus bathhouse. I Shazamed it discreetly and told no one lest Twitter finds out I support an appropriator.

In 2021, a popular TikToker named Addison Rae, who amassed one of the highest follower counts in its history, appeared on *The Tonight Show Starring Jimmy Fallon*. Fallon himself has his own racy history with blackface and race. In baggy pants stomping in white Air Force Ones like Nelly, Addison did a dance challenge, the Renegade—which is typically performed to a sound byte of K Camp's "Lottery." She smiled, bowed, and collected her flowers from the

American white majority. A fourteen-year-old Jalaiah Harmon watched unheard. Somewhere, someone uploads a clip of aged singer Cilla Black in a red blazer saying she made Dionne Warwick's "Anyone Who Had a Heart" more commercial in a way that undermines what others might call blatant stealing and appropriation.

The 1960s were not short of artists covering one another's music. It was something of a tradition to do a cover and accompany it with a rearrangement to put one's own spin on to the music. However, global white audiences and the businesses who provided the audiences the sound rarely translated the profit and notoriety these cover artists received to the first talent to perform this music. Likewise, the art was not always reimagined enough to differentiate one artist's sound from the cover artist's.

Dionne Warwick grew up in an arts period of her own. At the time, your sound and songs and your technique were how you fed your family. Many artists were willing to die for a song to call their own as penned by a songwriter worth their steep price. A good song with great talent was how Black artists crossed over and made more than the pennies most musicians at the time took home.

The only threat you faced was that song being taken and outperformed by someone less than, or worse, more.

Less ugly. Less dark. Less country. Less soulful. More beautiful. More metropolitan. More mainstream. More white.

The history of the song "Anyone Who Had a Heart" is a lot more complicated than a song intended for Dionne too. Cher was the first one to reap commercial success with the song before Dionne Warwick got a hold of it. But it was still something personal that a Black woman got her hands on it, did something original to its performance and found her audience enrichened for it.

And it felt personal that Dionne Warwick was so quickly discarded by the public when Cilla was given the song after her and, to Warwick, did nothing original with it. A story lost its happily ever after and gained a cautionary tale. Black kids have oh so many cautionary tales.

I think about the meaning of the word "challenge" on social media. It's a competition of sorts, but no one says if it is of skill or of notoriety or what. It cannot be skill because Jalaiah Harmon is clearly the better dancer. The side-by-sides prove it. And, while art is subjective, dance and style have technical points that impress skill and familiarity with what you are doing. People assume Black dance and art does not, but it does. The passion is a part of the performance. The bravado is a part of the performance. The groove is a part of the performance. Black American dance is African dance, and African dance has a call and response.

Perhaps it is notoriety then that these challenges are asking for young Black dancers to participate in. But then we are having a conversation on race, no? Because fame in America is a racialized lottery. Black creators must be mindful of their voices, mindful of our presence. Our peace is dictated by the comfort of this third space where whiteness of any race can rest. We must be the comfortable kind of people where ethnic tourism is not only encouraged, but entirely the point. There's not a lot of room in places like this for activism. Ain't a lot of space for you to be dangerous about your anger.

That same year of 2021, another TikToker named Erick Lewis or @Theericklouis (1.1 million TikTok followers) started a tongue-in-cheek boycott for Black TikTokers. In his call to action, there would be no new dance videos and no new dance choreography. The challenges would come to a grinding halt and the wheel of cultivation that drives their algorithms would rust. TikTok more than any other app is aware of how Black creators run the algorithm. Young Jalaiah Harmon pioneered some of the best dance trends on the app, having been robbed just months before Addison Rae went on Jimmy Fallon, but had not garnered equal attention. Likewise, Moanabih (1.6 million TikTok followers) and her dance friends put themselves to the effort of honing and mastering the complex ballad of vogue and its five essential elements in the hallway of their performance arts high school. Where were their talk show appearances? Where were their heavy-duty campaigns?

Erick Lewis's content involved itself heavily in Black and queer liberation. One of his most iconic videos is a mukbang—a taste test—featuring flavored condoms. He's discussed in the past how this on its own prevents him from a lot of the more profitable opportunities among influence as an entertainment industry. Most influencers are salesmen and don't hide it. There's always a hustle or a brand deal. Not so much a sponsor, but actual content featuring and starring something they want to sell to you. Erick Lewis is a dancer on his own right, too, but he focused on creating content and building a platform discussing and calling in blatant anti-Blackness, queerphobia, and transgressions against Black culture. In the time since his boycott and the many videos he made where he featured a new song—clearly targeting the stream bait that is TikTok—and made absolutely no motion. Not a wobble. Not an isolation. He stared right into the camera, his own sort of challenge, and demanded that the non-Black majority of the app do something creative for once.

I've come to understand what TikTok means by a dance challenge by how you can fail it. By being incapable of moving without the Black people showing you how.

HOT TAKE

I crossed a thousand followers by think-piecing on Twitter.

As I type this, my writing prompt underlines that verb and calls me incorrect. Oxford ain't really concerned with getting the freestyle rules of the Black dialects. That word only goes where it flows and flow it will toward the intent and impact, rather than the doddering rule of prescription.

I'll left click the prompt to teach the prompt that this verb is a word. I'll explain to anyone else that this word means many things. It means to think through written form, and it means to educate, and it means to lecture, and it means to get some things wrong, but that isn't always the point. It means to learn as you go, but always with a source of expertise. It means to be skilled. It means to be flawed. It means to be open to wounding from any old motherfucker with a login credential and the gumption to type out a witty crass remark.

It means troublemaker, peace executioner, brave and bold, sharp-tongued and outspoken. It means other. It means intellectual. It means that shit ain't right in the community and now we need to set it back on course.

When I say I crossed the thousand-followers mark on Twitter by think-piecing, I mean I made a lot of people upset. I got into fights and learned a fighter's exhaustion.

I remember telling a friend I made online that fighting online is a warfare of the psychic nature. You throw your full attention into the blue light. Your eyes sear and burn, and your fingers smack soft, smooth glass or glance soft, thin cracks until cuts interrupt your thumb groove's maps.

In 2014, Blue Ivy Carter was one of the most hated babies on the face of the earth. I imagine what is being done spiritually when a child so young is being so illfully discussed by people who should be old enough to know better. Who should be able to be quiet where the issue involves someone barely old enough to lift on their own. It is not me saying this in defense of capitalism, because I've been online long enough to know that capitalism is something that mires conversations on how we should talk about Beyoncé or her kin.

Most of the people attacked Blue Ivy with desire. That is with the tool that people don't know they know all about: where people's bodies have a value assigned upon it based on conditions that have nothing to do with the honesty of the body or history. It says that a Black girl should look as little like her daddy as possible while never looking too far away in that people could question that baby's legitimacy. That a Black girl's nose should not be too wide or dark or curved at the horn up the brim of their nose. Black boys have to be buff, not soft or round. Our bodies chiseled as much as it can be managed with tools that are as rustic as what I've seen.

They'd been responding to her paparazzi photos over anything else. Since the day that doctors almost committed crimes on their title to catch a look at the most famous baby on the planet and Beyoncé had to fight for something as casual and ordinary as privacy.

Eventually, the girl would completely disappear except for a few odd cameos and features where she showed the talent and precision of a millionaire mother. But her name is synonymous with the ill-filled gaze one is centered in when perception overrides your reality. It is the same filter that covers Chrissy Teigen when she condemns the young *Annie* actress Qvenzhané Wallis's name in a string of tweets—though Teigen would later apologize, but an "I'm sorry" does so little for the culture this action perpetuates.

In October 2015, Zola aka A'Ziah King posted the 148-tweet-story thread about a wild trip she took to Florida with a new stripper-friend named Jessica, whom she met while working at a restaurant. It was the first of its kind. The story had everything: Nigerian pimps, tiny dicks, big dicks, the proper puissance of pussy, a suicidal boyfriend, failed female empowerment, murder, and an underlying horror when one realizes the heart of the story is a Black woman who was attempted to be sex trafficked by her said "friends." It was just a single spotlight into the life and horror of sex workers back in a period where they only had their own cunning to protect themselves and one another. A phrase manifests around such a topic involving sex workers on the internet: "canaries in a coal mine." Politicians use sex workers as test subjects for what they can get away with in the public eye. They also use prisoners, but that conversation is lumped into what most think they can get away with people they typically also engage. In this viral conversation, we saw many people react and exaggerate what happened to Zola, ignoring the parts of the tale that was a woman trying to peddle her friend. She wasn't human. She was content in a warping of Nora Ephron's iconic quote, where everything is content.

Eventually, Zola's story became a movie. They found a way to capture the magical realism of not only Zola, but of the social media platform Zola used to tell the story. Even when she is silent on the screen, it is fixated on her: what she has to say, how she reacts, the health of her point of view. It's the first time the digital story is told in this way, and you can feel Zola's expertise there: the betrayal of this girl, but also the good nature of a girl who sees a victim in this little white girl who tried to sabotage her because she herself doesn't know she was sabotaged.

It's a film that could've gone a different direction if Zola wasn't also in the room controlling the story. It wouldn't be the first time someone forgot the human involved in what we are talking about.

To be viral is to lose some semblance of your humanity to those who spread you. Much like COVID-19 or HIV, you are no longer the individual virus comprising one body. Not the ancestry of biological assaults, not the cocktail of thermonuclear accidents within the cellular membrane. You are instead a cosmology. An idea. COVID killed your meemaw, not the respiratory infections that comprise such a monumental shut down of the bodies' immune system. AIDS killed your uncle, because it is a lot easier to embody such a sickness in words and not the shocking narrative of blister sores and cracked lips or gray filmed eyes. Not the countless CD4 cells perishing in a war within your body. You become fodder for another's lifestream. One that might die if you do as well. The hope in the end is that it lives long enough to become a part of that imaginary greater consciousness—where the hate umbrellas your one fate in a party of philosophy.

10

No Justice. No peace.

—A BLACK REVOLUTIONARY

SUMMER OF FREEDOM

As I write this in the last three weeks of June 2020, I have been sub-ject to more Black pain than I have ever cared to witness. I have felt the reverb of my siblings across the planet—sheltering in the base of my spinal cord, coiling under my rib cage. It pricks me between my shoulder blades. I cannot sleep for long. I wake up wheezing, gasping. The air is not plentiful. There is pain everywhere. It is in my double helix like double dutch, or a lynching rope, or the continent my mother traced across her thigh when she decreed she'd be queen of a far-off country shaped exactly like it. It is the flavor of my blood.

George Floyd
Breonna Taylor
Tony McDade
Oluwatoyin Salau

I have a wound for each of them: festering like cancer. And yet I cannot pull myself away from the screens. I must drown myself in their suffering to keep their memories alive. It's like all Blackness is or will ever be is pain.

For a day, I lay in my bed knotted together by a thin sheet. I've rolled so often onto my left side, my right side, that my pillowcase has crumbled beneath my neck, providing no support. The shadow of racism haunts me no matter where I turn. Music turns into dry sand in my ears, and it fills me with nothing but the uncomfortable gradient:

I could be doing something about this right now.

Three weeks ago, I lay witness to the greatest atrocity I could ever imagine outside of Black bodies lying cold or navy blue on a sidewalk. My timelines grind to a halt as Black art dies for solidarity with George Floyd. Days later, a media wide #Blackout is called to bolster awareness throughout the industries. Instead, the #BlackLivesMatter channels are congested with large black squares that serve to silence. Black thought has gone empty. And I'm in hell.

The internet is a cruel place to put your energy. It is a spiritual attack that you subscribe to every time you log on—if that can be the word to describe what takes place. Black folk never really log on to social media after the millennials got ahold of the technology. You press a button, as casual as you are walking down the street. However, it has the same perils. Stay on your toes, because many people might be the main character of the day, but only Black folk can be the villains.

Too loud.

Too soft.

Too unspecified.

The only difference between real life and the internet is that online you can still heal. That's what Black art has always been about, after all: healing. A week ago, I marched at the Columbus state house to protest with the friends I've made marching into my Blackness, and I'd forgotten how to heal.

I do not know if it had much to do with the silence, those black squares—so empty of color, matching one another. They looked so completely still: so deep, like you could fall into them and be forgotten. And you could scream names out to the world above—your name, and where you stay and the people you love, but it'd be drowned out. And nothing you did would reach the top.

When the world is that bleak, it's almost necessary to forget how to heal. Healing is what people do when they believe in tomorrow. Creation is an investment in the future, after all. Black folk have been doing it for years. You sing on a plantation because you know rest will come. You dance through Jubilee because the shackles don't pin you down. You write through Jim Crow because words are your power. You do it all, because tomorrow is worth healing for.

But, then, George Floyd dies. Someone posts his death for us all to see; they show us our brother stolen in the midst of a quarantine—proving to us all that even while humanity fights against pestilence, and the Earth shrinks its population virtually by the hundred thousands, Black life is not worth preserving. It's not worth the shine of a second's thought. And it shows us that healing maybe isn't enough. That tomorrow's sun is not worth today's dim.

And, thus, the art dies out. Good night, it slumbers.

//////////

While we were marching for Black men in the streets, many things can go on at once. An immaculate series of gears moving in the machine of the heart. There is no grinding, as such would suggest such abrupt friction that there is disharmony. There is no whirring as such would suggest an inhumane seamlessness that is something some might expect if were believed in the disreputable respectability that is Black folk of a Cosby generation.

There is a rhythm as improvised as the music we come to love. Something so worth doing that it cannot be planned. When Black folk were marching for Black men, they were dancing, too—a video goes viral of a duo krumping in the face of the police. We mocked it. A Black man in a shiny white tee thrusting for his life in the face of armed white men with bullets that render even the most indestructible passion, including dance, frantically mortal. At the same time, Atlanta's most wealthy, who called for an end to the violence and the attacks on their favorite shops, were pincushions to the severity of our rages. Black elite called for our anger to be silenced for their capital. That Black business ought to be indestructible. That white business with Black business ought to be indestructible. That white business with white business, but Black brand deals, ought to be indestructible. Trina called BLM protesters animals.[1] The late Virgil Abloh gave a paltry $50 to the (F)empower Community Bond Fund in Miami; he was laughed at and gave more to the song of $20,500.[2]

At the same time, Noname twote a rallying cry for Black elite and entertainers to follow our predecessors: the artists of the Black Power Movement. To take the capital we earned by platforming Black art to the masses.

The masses echoed her sentiment in kind with an immortalized chant: "Open your purse."[3]

Spotify and Amazon stood with Black Lives, and Twitter pointed out the hypocrisy of two union-busting megacorps standing with Black Lives in police violence all while neglecting Black people providing the means of their production. Careers were made and broken by a quick realization of how serious we've become as a people commercialized and exploited: that if a platitude is gonna be empty, it should at least come with a signed check.

On December 21, 2020, Black folk gained superpowers. The weeks prior, creators recorded themselves in varying stages of apotheosis. X-genes exploded in the veins of Black men and women. The air straining around them. Their eyes pushing the back of their skulls until the nerves bit. Others speculated, which is a fancy word for "dreamed," about what their great talent might be.

A comic nerd myself, I had names for the abilities these Black folk were looking for. I had an idea, while most people thought we would all get our own individual abilities. I thought we'd get something more like a Kryptonian—a grab bag of greatness in our blood.

There's the common abilities I think all Black folk might have. Hypermobility. Black telepathy. Preternatural hindsight. But then there's the grand and new ability: the supernatural talent of visibility. To be seen, to be heard, to be felt.

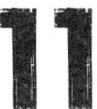

11

I ain't gotta do shit but stay Black and survive.

—A BLACK DREAMER

UPHEAVAL IN THE COURT

In 2023, just after the entertainment industry danced on the tip of a needle's forehead, a TikTok influencer says that it is better to have a white audience over a Black one because a Macy's campaign was not exactly selling as well as she might've hoped. She accused another prominent influencer, a young Black woman named Fannita, of relying on a marginally white audience to build her career. Black content creators did not take kindly to her saying that. Most everyone refused to buy anything she was selling, literally and figuratively, a problem because she was advertising a Target line of kitchenware. It's kind of a boycott, if you squint and realize the chances of folk buying this was proportionate to the care people had in the face of the brand.

That same year, a real protest shook the foundation of the artist economy both offline and online.

March 7, 2023, over 90 percent of writers among the Writers Guild of America (WGA) agreed that they wanted better conditions. On one part, it was about compensation and residuals for screenwriters in the new culture of streaming and television. On another part, it was about preemptively escalating protection against a film and TV industry that was increasingly reliant on artificial intelligence technology to cut costs. Negotiations began, but by May 2, the WGA was fully on strike.

By July, SAG-AFTRA began its strike. I was on-set waiting for an actor to show up to record a podcast episode. She didn't show. During this time, social media was abuzz with questions of what did or didn't qualify a violation of boycott requests and picket lines.

Content creators questioned whether their careers put them with industry professionals or made them categorically the exception to so many obligations of boycotts. Some Black creators suggested this was the only opportunity for larger brands to finally pay attention to platforms largely overlooked despite their numbers and talent. Over the course of the 2010s, entertainment started relying on content creators more for marketing opportunities for films and television. For content creators, it was a quid pro quo: creators got to be legitimized in the eyes of entertainment by being seen or present on red carpets or in their press junkets. Black creators were not always let into these spaces—not without heavy competition, at least.

From my understanding, there were some ideas that the entertainment industry's needs did not need to be considered because the entertainment industry routinely disregarded Black creators. There are some merits to this. Even Hilliard Guess, cochair of the WGA West's Committee of Black Writers, observed fears that the job market for Black screenwriters would shrink.[1] Even after the George Floyd protests and the resulting surge in diversity interest, the projects centering people of color and Black stories did not equate to an equality of wages. Some Black creators observed that not many non-Black actors and writers brought this up prior to the strike, when they could profit off this inequity in wages.

Nonetheless, Black writers and actors took to social media to push audiences to resist the urge to support other people who had lost their damn minds: Alliance of Motion Picture and Television Producers (AMPTP).

The writers won in the end. The actors . . . got something they could maybe live with if they're lucky. But what was charted during this fight was how much revolved around Black creators—content creators and artists of the digital space—were pushed to one side or another. AMPTP tried to replace the potential advertising they could get from actors pushing their shows on red carpets, talk shows, and more by having fandoms engage in scabbing. The workers—actors, writers, and other artists—expected these creators to hold the line. The assumption was that many of these people—like those whose come-up was largely by chance—would have no aspiration of being "real" artists. That they'd never want to join a creator's guild.

They were incorrect.

They also suggested that they could outwait the suffering of these creatives' families.

To be wrong twice so publicly was bound to impact their self-esteem.

And, worse, the entertainment industry found out how unwilling even the individuals whose interest in content creation was specifically involved with community could not or would not stomach betraying the communal interest.

Perhaps it was because most of the viewers regarded the publishers of their favorite content as liars. During the 2023 Summer of Freedom, many organizations, companies, and businesses made bold promises to the public and the artists they loved. #PublishingPaidMe revealed the grotesque inequalities facing Black authors and writers when it came to the financial compensation some of the most iconic and lauded Black creatives of our generation earned. Case studies also discovered that most of the entertainment industry was horribly segregated. Black minds, workers, and leadership composed less than 5 percent of the *overall* industry. Netflix laid off most of its Strong Black Lead content team; Max canceled a string of Black television and film projects; Disney canceled queer programming left and right upon the rise of new, overwhelming leadership.

The Black community had expectations of its new industry that was also not being met across diversity and inclusion initiatives. And posting a Black square would not save them from the quite evident deceptions under the name of corporate DEI.

There used to be a way of doing things on this app that understood what morbid curiosity was all about. We could make jokes about the potential of our own deaths and oppression because we made jokes together. When the "Nigger Navy" sailed or when we inched closer and closer to doomsday, something could be funny, as if we were laughing at the idea of a Black future not being forever. We were together in the preposterousness of this. If no one had us, we had us.

The village voice held a unified front. It was the last unified front.

Y'ALL WANNA HEAR A STORY ABOUT WHY WE AND THIS B*TCH TWITTER FELL OUT?

In 2022, I moved to Los Angeles to start a new job in advertising but also to get into a new headspace as I started the next chapter of my life as a writer.

I was no longer just a digital anything. That story, that narrative, had to be left behind.

The world was different from what it was in 2019 when folk really cared about the communities they brought up. I'd been blacklisted back then, but it'd been worth it. I'd looked up to people and it hadn't been.

I was outspoken about a lot, and now I struggled to find something worth burning for in my pen that was worth the lashings I got. Our arena had crowded full of people. I couldn't stretch my arms out far enough and find someone willing to help me do something just on here. Not even for the sake that we were neighbors.

In Los Angeles, folk can give you a lot of room to stretch. You can hit the ends of your joints and still not brush another bit of flesh.

And you get more room the more you become a cog just grinding on and on and on until the clink of metal becomes a smooth sawing of flat-round on flatter-round.

You can touch nothing but cold air and what exactly went wrong.

Black Bird was an effort by Jack Dorsey to give credit, attention, and safety to the Black users of Twitter who had pioneered his product into a community of strong-minded and strong-willed changemakers. It was made on the back of years of questions on the safety policies revolving around the Black people who populated the app and the Black women who stewarded that exact same place; it was also made to reflect the over policing of Black users of the app by those same moderator bots and persons.

The first of the major offenses: we couldn't say "Nigga."

Strike one.

The word is filled with controversy, I get it. But the suspensions of accounts who fought their hardest to support the way of doing things on Twitter was a bit much. For one, the humor of Black Twitter is about finding a line and throwing a party behind it. In the olden days, before Tumblr crashed and users flooded the TL, some suggested it was a bit more overt and riskier, but it was self-aware enough to know that being the eternal clown is really about waiting for the laughter to die and for your head to be on the chopping block.

In Black people, it evokes potent reactions. I think it's a bit uppity to make a big deal about it, but still I allow Black people to decide their own paths and respect it. Niggas have been speaking on niggas not because they don't love them, but because it's the best word to describe a sensation and an understanding of community. It can be a nasty word, maybe among the most vulgar in the English language. But it isn't the worst one, because the language is one of conquerors and the colonized. And it is also a word that best showcases the truth that racism has no one fixed form, that it cares more about the who than the what. Niggas don't really care when niggas are niggas. Black people do care when non-niggas try to frame us like that. There's a line of understanding where the race ends and racism begins, and it works. So, I wonder why in knowing do we find our language policed, controlled, and propped on its toes like a marionette.

The app treated every Black person performing the art of language like equal criminals. The sad part is, the true racists had a way of skirting the lines of the Twitter community guidelines. I've seen monkey emojis and bananas; I've seen questions on my "nickers" and my "n1gg9as." In spaces like these, racism becomes netting holding up the walls. It takes intricate knots to secure the place.

Strike two.

Elon Musk bought the Twitter app in 2022 and, since then, things have gone to shit. Prior to the acquisition, Twitter was preparing for something more. I was one of a string of creators verified under a new initiative by Twitter to start looking for the native creators with something to offer—whether in humor, ethics, or education—that could populate the timeline and trending section with creative expression and voice. My blue check came just after my Twitter account was suspended (on a permanent basis allegedly) for DMCA violations. I never really posted a music video: I'm not a Napster. I was posting memes. Some of them had music in them—maybe about fifteen seconds worth of sound. When Kamala Harris won the 2020 election alongside President Joe Biden, I overlayed KRS-One's "Sound of da Police" to Harris's victory strut. The joke was that Kamala Harris was a cop. She participated in the empire's carceral system during her time as the district attorney of San Francisco. The joke used the fact that the DA's office obtained more than 1,900 convictions for marijuana offenses, which included the kinds of convictions padded onto serious crimes. Harris's prosecution rate exceeded her predecessors. And while the number of defendants sentenced to state prison was also lower, the energy of a pro-reform general Black public left a smear on her legacy. While Harris could be seen through liberal eyes as a well-meaning politician, the political aspect of her behavior made her largely unsavory. It didn't quite make her an Uncle Tom, but it definitely made her like a cop and that's not bad enough to lose an election, but it's bad enough to make you the center of some hilarious jokes.

When I returned to my main account, I returned to a revitalized approach to my social media. I've been loud criticizing blue checks, because a lot of the blue check culture seemed to be against what was really going on in these spaces. A lot of the conversations with the people who were the perpetually online, opening conversations of advancing Blackness, on leftist ideas, on the corruption that celebrity can sometimes entail, were ignored for marketing, capital, and the worldbuilding of empire. We were not fooled when we saw writers, thought leaders, and the powerful of the entertainment industry populating Twitter, talking as if they were "one of us" while rejecting proximity to the people they followed and whose access to the same resources they casually use to pay their bills were limited. People joined online spaces for community to find people who made their existence just a bit more bearable because their physical realities did not reflect this. And if they didn't mock these users, this community who made apps like Twitter what they were, they saw them as temporary echoes following their grand legends. The concept of a blue check entailed a detachment from the conversations surrounding the people in question. I was not of the people who used Jack Dorsey's app, until the keys to the kingdom were handed out.

Before Elon Musk purchased the app, Twitter launched huge campaigns focusing on uplifting its creators. #TweetItIntoExistence spotlighted talent throughout Twitter's existence who cultivated brilliant and widely celebrated careers in the arts. Matthew A. Cherry crowdfunded *Hair Love* on Twitter and moved on to win an Oscar, a testament to the independent power waiting on Twitter if publishers were to properly activate and listen to the individuals who made their power in this community.

It wasn't just Matthew A. Cherry either. They shared on bill-boards Niall Horan's X *Factor* application tweet; they shared Demi Lovato declaring that they would sing the national anthem at the Super Bowl one day; they showed what Megan Thee Stallion thought of herself as a rapper before she finished college; the *Awkward Black Girl* herself, Issa Rae, declaring that she would be a more successful version of herself.

During the campaign, I met virtually with a representative from Twitter at my sister's kitchen table to discuss the goals of the new content creator initiative. They wanted to advertise me. They wanted to market my book. They wanted to create a space where all artists felt bold enough to let their work live on this app that could be negative but could also become lucrative if it had the ambition. There were many tools for Twitter that were locked behind a blue check, and now they were going to become mine—and, eventually, for everyone who thought that Twitter could become a new YouTube.

And then Elon Musk purchased Twitter on October 27, 2022. Some say he didn't even really want to do it. A flex went just a little too far.

Once he took over the app, Black Bird shut down. Musk laid off the representative, along with every hope-weaver employed by the company. What he replaced them with were the people he felt would give him the most effort for a vision some—like me—would call mad.

Strike three.

The community died.

There is no romance to the language of such a situation. XLNB, the Emmy-nominated filmmaker and forerunner of Twitter story-telling, would have a better way to talk about this type of stuff. We don't have to think any of his stories were real: that's the wonder of hyperbole. The exaggeration of the truth to erect the truth rather than the honest. What happens does not matter to a story, after all, what people remember to tell again does.

If XLNB had left today, when the community died, I imagine he'd have talked about it as the day friends turned against friends and the ones too young to be scrolling the timeline a decade ago learned the wrong lessons. He'd describe it with something near parable like a pastor: the seeds of the poisoned fruit. He'd try to connect to them with his last dying breath—to flee the habit of outrage with any random person who diverges from this idea that people are content, rather than the things they put out. He'd call for the spaces to end, at least on the frequency they do. He'd ask for commentary to have a substantive structure: a beginning, a middle, and an end that at least acknowledges agreements, allies, and consistent angsts.

But XLNB left the app years ago when his role as a director became a lot more substantial. We haven't had a story time with him in quite some time. And when storytellers flee, some believe that is when the village voice departs, because who will teach us what is worth telling again if there is no one to remember what was worth forgetting?

When I left the app—most apps—I did so when the story had run stale. One more beef. One more argument. One more negativity. When my name had been smeared again, or a lie went too far. Not when it was one more Black body painting gray sidewalks red, not when my sisters fought another misogynist whose words carried an army to her presence. It was when I felt no more community, the kind of kin who chide you with loving in the words. When I stopped typing because I found something beautiful my siblings could behold and found only one more day of awful and not shelter away from the way it smelled.

I couldn't think of any new names, then. No new people here who were worth the time it'd take to feel . . . disappointment in what they put into the world. Not a conversation that sparked. Not a portrait that wasn't cheapened by intelligence not their own. Not an effort to do.

The movement once meant that if anything could be copy, it could also be a story—an art designed to transform. And we had run out of things to say that we had not said before.

RENAISSANCE

Beyoncé announced a renaissance to open her new era of music. It was filled with Black queer art and celebration. A jubilee of sensation, shimmer, and shine. We vogued for nights and twirled. We became deviants at circuit parties and encouraged ourselves to hold hands in broad daylight. We understood our humanity could be complicated and made art on art and talked about the things that could bring a bit more art into our lives off this digital plane.

O'Shea Sibley was murdered at a gas station trying to live that everyday truth. The grief that flowed out of me was piping, forming figure eights above steeping drinks. His last grand act was performance art in celebration of a moment, cut short by one act of resistance to things blurring across the lines of what they were told could be.

If I had to define Black art, it's Inglewood at a flea market. Orchestrated portraits of dark-skinned Black men in cornrows in white beaters and dark-skinned women with gold-painted dangling earrings three inches from another man arguing the white man's evil of homosexuality. It's complicated, like color contrast, like sepia on a summer day. It's performance and the truths we juggle and the lies that make those truths bearable.

The internet made a new form of performance art out of Black hustle. In it, the only way Black people get paid is sometimes giving a corner to the white people who have the money. A juggle, a struggle.

This is a renaissance of how we sell ourselves and what it does to the space afterward. The ways it enrichens the fingers and the soil. The faster ways it poisons the fruit and the farm. It's a commodity of a YouTube age, where everything on a box within a box is for sale if you have a bio with an electronic blue mark across a string of acronyms and sentence fragments.

But, on the flip side, renaissance is not always so cut and dry. It's sometimes a challenge to the world as a whole: What radical things can happen for free when Black people are simply given a space to be?

With all the details, we could all probably survive. We can all probably smile through the pain for a second.

ACKNOWLEDGMENTS

Forever for the Culture started as a pitch to my mentor Terron Moore, then vice president of MTV News, as a column. I wanted to create a portrait for Black art that memorialized the modern as Black history. I also wanted to keep my phone bill paid, and columns for digital and culture journalists were guaranteed monthly checks. Terron, with infinite patience, did not destroy the idea altogether. He simply corrected my direction. This idea was huge, but it was too huge for a column.

Black history is a circuit of valuable words given to Black people in small, seemingly trivial moments. Remember your moments before you go off to sleep: they are all valuable. Thank you, Eric Smith, for being the only champion I could hope for with my book. To Maya Fernandez, thank you for rocking with the vision and tending the soil from which my book grew. To the wonderful people at Beacon Press, thank you for not cringing at my social media presence and remembering there is a writer underneath the chaotic posting. To my subjects Tré, Franchesca, and Kenny, you were all so amazing.

This book is also an altar to my family and friends. Thank you, Grandma Maureen "Kandy Kane" Fluellen, for planting a love in me that is so unconditional it will spread from here on out. It started with you; it will not end. Thank you, Tamara Fluellen, for the fiery pride in our people and the art others tell us is better off forgotten. Thank you, Van Collins, for teaching me I will be alright, even when you knew you'd never read my words in the end. To Robert Fluellen Jr., thank you for the love of whimsy—nothing is so serious that you can't be unserious. My sisters—Alexis and Corvetta—my eternal headaches: we are three. To Grandpa Robert "Flu" Fluellen, thank you for instilling in me wisdom. To Lonnie, thank you for resurrecting the music in our home.

To my friends: Mike, Brandon, Ricardo, Antwana, Jan, J.R., Paul, Keon, Moe, Dom. You sheltered my mind and heart; I will shelter you forever.

And to MarShawn McCarrel, thank you for being the first poet I've ever known. Thank you for being the only hero who would not let me down.

To the Black, beautiful, and ever-bettering: we will not just survive; we will thrive.

NOTES

CHAPTER 1

1. Taylor Lorenz, *Extremely Online: The Untold Story of Fame, Influence, and Power on the Internet*, Kindle ed. (New York: Simon & Schuster, 2023), 289.

2. Chanté Griffin, "How Natural Black Hair at Work Became a Civil Rights Issue," *JSTOR Daily*, July 3, 2019, https://daily.jstor.org/how-natural-black-hair-at-work-became-a-civil-rights-issue/.

3. Dale J. Cohen, Sheida White, and Steffaney B. Cohen, "Mind the Gap: The Black-White Literacy Gap in the National Assessment of Adult Literacy and Its Implications," *Journal of Literacy Research* 44, no. 2 (March 2012): 123–48, https://doi.org/10.1177/1086296X12439998.

4. Jon Caramanica, "The Gang That Brought High Fashion to Hip-Hop," *New York Times*, June 29, 2016, https://www.nytimes.com/2016/06/30/fashion/lo-lifes-fashion-hip-hop.html.

5. David Gonzalez, "Will Gentrification Spoil the Birthplace of Hip-Hop?" *New York Times*, May 21, 2007, https://www.nytimes.com/2007/05/21/nyregion/21citywide.html.

6. Steven Underwood, "Why the Bonds Between Straight Men Can Sometimes Sabotage Their Romantic Relationships," *Blavity News & Entertainment*, August 3, 2018, https://blavity.com/why-the-bonds-between-straight-men-can-sometimes-sabotage-their-romantic-relationships.

7. Griffin Dunne, dir., *Joan Didion: The Center Will Not Hold*, Netflix, 2017.

8. Abraham Josephine Riesman, "The Man Who Made Black Panther Cool," *Vulture*, January 22, 2018, https://www.vulture.com/2018/01/christopher-priest-made-black-panther-cool-then-disappeared.html.

CHAPTER 2

1. Taylor Lorenz, "The Problem with Shane Dawson and Jeffree Star: What Happened to These YouTube Stars?" *New York Times*, June 29, 2020, https://www.nytimes.com/2020/06/29/style/shane-dawson-jeffree-star-youtube-taylor-lorenz.html.

2. "Toni Morrison," *Charlie Rose*, PBS, May 7, 1993.

3. Khristina "Auzrielle" Raglin, "Mental Health in Black Adolescence: Dismissive Parents," *Medium*, February 1, 2021, https://medium.com/the-blak-lotus/mental-health-in-black-adolescence-dismissive-parents-5d17541a85fd.

CHAPTER 3

1. Mekado Murphy, "Viola Davis on What *The Help* Got Wrong and How She Proves Herself," *New York Times*, September 11, 2018, https://www.nytimes.com/2018/09/11/movies/viola-davis-interview-widows-toronto-film-festival.html.

2. Franchesca "Chescaleigh" Ramsey, interview by Steven Underwood, personal communication, September 5, 2023.

3. Mabinty Quarshie, "Eartha Kitt's Vietnam Comments Nearly Ended Her Career," *USA Today*, February 19, 2018, https://www.usatoday.com/story/news/nation-now/2018/02/16/eartha-kitt-and-lady-bird-johnson-vietnam/321602002/.

4. Academy Awards Acceptance Speech Database, Margaret Herrick Library, Academy of Motion Picture Arts & Sciences, https://aaspeechesdb.oscars.org/link/082–4/info.aspx, accessed April 13, 2024.

5. "Talking to Your Car/Hey Steve!/Harvey's Hundreds/Mo'Nique," *Steve*, season 2, episode 100, NBC, February 13, 2019.

6. "#blackhistory: On February 29, 1940, Hattie McDaniel Becomes the First Black Actor to Win an Academy Award," CAAM, https://caamuseum.org/learn/600state/black-history/blackhistory-on-february-29-1940-hattie-mcdaniel-becomes-the-first-black-actor-to-win-an-academy-award.

7. Mikhaela Jennings (@KHAENOTBAE), "I'm tryna see something #ROMWEnextgen #fyp #foryou #hair," TikTok, November 13, 2021, https://www.tiktok.com/@khaenotbae/video/7030125467613072646?lang=en.

8. Cecile Emeke, "Fake Deep (2014)," YouTube video, https://youtu.be/ikJoBiD7uDY?si=-7JwQEjgGenIc5aT, accessed January 14, 2025.

CHAPTER 4

1. Allison Cacich, "Is Lil Nas X Canceled? Rapper Accused of Writing Islamophobic Tweets," *Distractify*, March 30, 2021, https://www.distractify.com/p/lil-nas-x-canceled

2. Cacich, "Is Lil Nas X Canceled?"

3. Rodney Carmichael, "Wrangler on His Booty: Lil Nas X on the Making and the Magic of 'Old Town Road,'" NPR, April 10, 2019, https://www.npr.org/2019/04/10/711167412/wrangler-on-his-booty-lil-nas-x-on-the-making-and-the-magic-of-old-town-road.

4. Ben Dandridge-Lemco, "How an Uncredited German Producer's Free Loops Are Powering Platinum Rap Hits," *The FADER*, September 20, 2019, https://www.thefader.com/2019/09/20/minor2go-looperman-interview -polo-g-lil-tjay-loops.

5. Carl Lamarre, "'Old Town Road' Producer YoungKio on How Lil Nas X's Song Came to Life," *Billboard*, March 28, 2019, https://www .billboard.com/music/rb-hip-hop/old-town-road-producer-youngkio -interview-lil-nas-x-8504409/.

6. Stephen Daw, "Isaiah Rashad Comes Out as 'Sexually Fluid' After Leaked Sex Tape," *Billboard*, May 27, 2022, https://www.billboard.com /culture/pride/isaiah-rashad-sexually-fluid-joe-budden-sex-tape-1235078579/.

CHAPTER 5

1. Countee Cullen, "Heritage," *Color*, 1925.

2. Kenny Knox, personal interview on video chat, January 17, 2024.

CHAPTER 6

1. Quoted in Steven Underwood, "Luka Sabbat, We Need to Talk . . ." *Blaque Word*, September 6, 2018, https://blaqueword.wordpress.com/2018 /06/05/luka-sabbat-we-need-to-talk/.

CHAPTER 7

1. Brandy Zadrozny, "YouTube Tested, Trump Approved: How Candace Owens Suddenly Became the Loudest Voice on the Far Right," NBCNews.com, June 23, 2018, https://www.nbcnews.com/news/us-news /youtube-tested-trump-approved-how-candace-owens-suddenly-became -loudest-n885166.

2. Steven Underwood and Tré Melvin, personal interview on video chat, March 8, 2023.

3. Kimberlé Crenshaw, "Demarginalizing the Intersection of Race and Sex: A Black Feminist Critique of Antidiscrimination Doctrine, Feminist Theory, and Antiracist Politics," *University of Chicago Legal Forum*, vol. 1989, no. 8.

4. Steven Underwood and Tré Melvin, personal interview on video chat, March 8, 2023.

CHAPTER 8

1. Crazy Laugh Action, "Antoine Dodson 'Hide Yo Kids, Hide Yo Wife' Interview (Original)," YouTube video, 2:02, April 11, 2012, https:// youtu.be/EzNhaLUT520?si=gq9-QNWvdAyRJ-85.

2. Invisible Children, "Kony 2012," YouTube video, 29:58, March 5, 2012, https://youtu.be/Y4MnpzG5Sqc?si=oaudRLwyud5rPgx9.

3. *TMZ*, "'Hide Your Kids' Star Antoine Dodson Speaks on 'Digital Blackface,'" YouTube video, 2:39, March 28, 2023, https://youtu.be /mDXHvTFjRwI?si=USL8xf2Ek51Ryfny.

4. Erin McLaughlin, "'On Fleek' Inventor Kayla Newman AKA Peaches Monroee on Her Beauty Line," *Teen Vogue*, March 9, 2017, https://www.teenvogue.com/story/on-fleek-inventor-kayla-newman-aka -peaches-monroe-on-her-beauty-line.

5. "Donate to Peaches Cosmetic & Hair Line, Organized by Kayla Lewis," Gofundme.com, February 19, 2017, https://www.gofundme.com /f/peaches-cosmetic-hair-line.

6. BET, "What 'Eyebrows On Fleek' Creator Peaches Monroee Learned the Hard Way—I Went Viral," YouTube video, 4:38, September 19, 2018, https://www.youtube.com/watch?v=KbI-CXZAoNw.

7. Landon Romano (@LandonRomano), "I'm only going to say this one more time. what you see of me online is pretty much who I am in real life. My accent and my attitude is just who I am. I'm from," Twitter (now X), July 2, 2018, https://x.com/landonromano/status/1013913895205916672.

8. Landon Romano (@LandonRomano), "YOUR BITCH JUST GOT PAID AYYYYYEEE FINNA GET THIS HAIR DID," Twitter (now X), September 8, 2014, https://x.com/landonromano/status/509069290889568256.

9. Landon Romano (@LandonRomano), "Black people invented the music industry. And that's just facts," Twitter (now X), February 13, 2020, https://x.com/landonromano/status/1228150714876084224.

10. Landon Romano (@LandonRomano), "Black people won this race for us period," Twitter (now X), November 7, 2020, https://x.com/landon romano/status/1325123274779488256.

11. Landon Romano (@LandonRomano), "A black women just got elected as Vice President 🎉🎉🎉 History has just been made. I'm crying," Twitter (now X), November 7, 2020, https://x.com/landonromano/status /1325120046037782544.

12. Landon Romano (@LandonRomano), "I don't give a fuck who looting out of target or whatever the fuck. there is a bigger picture here," Twitter (now X), May 27, 2020, https://x.com/landonromano/status /1265866251043090432.

13. Landon Romano (@LandonRomano), "NOT ALL BLACK WOMEN ACT ALIKE. NOT ALL WHITE WOMEN ACT LIKE. NOT ALL WHITE MEN ACT LIKE," Twitter (now X), December 17, 2018, https://x.com/landonromano/status/1074632553036898304.

14. Landon Romano (@LandonRomano), "As grateful as I am for the overwhelming amount of brand deal offers I have received," Twitter (now X), November 19, 2018, https://x.com/landonromano/status /1064700969940746241.

CHAPTER 10

1. *Vibe*, "Trina Apologizes for Comments About Protestors After Receiving Backlash," June 4, 2020, https://www.vibe.com/news/entertainment /trina-apology-comments-about-protestors-681231/.

2. Xavier Hamilton, "Virgil Abloh Responds to Criticism over $50 Donation to Protesters' Bail Fund," *Complex*, June 1, 2020, https://www .complex.com/style/a/fnr-tigg/virgil-abloh-responds-criticism-50-dollar -donation-protesters-bail-fund.

3. Kamilah Gumbs, "Opinion: Open Your Purse," *The Sunflower*, June 24, 2020, https://thesunflower.com/51572/opinion/opinion-open-your -purse/.

CHAPTER 11

1. Jevon Phillips, "Striking Black Screenwriters Fear the Job Market Will Shrink," *Los Angeles Times*, September 22, 2023, https://www.latimes .com/entertainment-arts/business/story/2023-09-22/writers-strike-wga -black-writers-contraction-hollywood-hiring.